Education Gone Wild

The Rise of Forest Schools

Around the World

Julia Gayle

CONTENTS

Introduction

"Look deep into nature, and then you will understand everything better."
- Albert Einstein

The wisdom in Einstein's words rings as a profound echo across the ages, a reminder that in the embrace of nature lies the clarity to comprehend the world in its entirety. This assertion, simple yet revolutionary, serves as the cornerstone of a movement that is reshaping the educational landscape around the globe: the rise of forest schools.

Why, one might wonder, does this connection between nature and understanding carry such weight? And how does it relate to the education of our youngest citizens? The answer lies not just in the cognitive benefits that outdoor learning environments provide but in the fundamental reconnection of human beings with the natural world—a bond that has been frayed by the relentless march of urbanization and technological advancement.

At the heart of this book lies a challenge: to rethink the conventional walls-and-windows model of schooling. Standardized testing and strict curriculum in conventional schools can obscure students' individual growth and development. But as we venture into the forest, among the whispering trees and the soft hum of the natural world, a different kind of learning unfolds—one that nurtures creativity, resilience, and a profound sense of stewardship for the earth.

My journey into the heart of forest schooling is not just an academic endeavor. Living amidst the serene beauty of the forest, I have witnessed firsthand the transformation that occurs when children are allowed to explore, to play, and to learn under the canopy of trees. The forest becomes a classroom without borders, where lessons are not dictated by textbooks but are discovered through the curious eyes of children as they interact with their surroundings.

As we delve deeper into the essence of forest schools, we unravel a narrative that is both ancient and urgently contemporary. From their roots in the Scandinavian outdoor tradition of friluftsliv to the burgeoning network of forest kindergartens and outdoor educational programs around the world, forest schools represent a paradigm shift. They challenge the assumption that learning can only happen within the four walls of a classroom and offer an alternative that is as expansive as the open sky.

But what makes the forest school philosophy so revolutionary? It's the recognition that education is not just about imparting knowledge but about fostering a lifelong relationship with learning—and with the planet we call home. This book intends to illuminate the myriad ways in which forest schools are not only cultivating a generation of informed and environmentally conscious individuals but are also rekindling a collective sense of wonder for the natural world.

Your curiosity, dear reader, is a testament to the growing awareness of the importance of this bond with nature. It is an indication that the seeds of change are already taking root within us, urging us to look beyond the conventional and to envision a future where education is a vibrant, living entity, intertwined with the earth itself.

Imagine a world where children grow up understanding the language of trees, where the rhythm of the seasons guides the learning process, and where the earth is revered as the ultimate teacher. This is the world that forest schools are striving to create—a world where nature and education walk hand in hand toward a sustainable and enlightened future.

As we stand at the threshold of this exciting journey, one question beckons: Are we ready to step into the forest and rediscover the essence of learning?

The chapters that follow will guide you through the verdant path of this educational revolution, offering insights, stories, and the promise of a world transformed by the power of nature. Together, we will explore the origins, the challenges, and the triumphs of forest schools around the world.

And perhaps, in the whisper of the leaves and the murmur of the streams, we will find the answers that we seek.

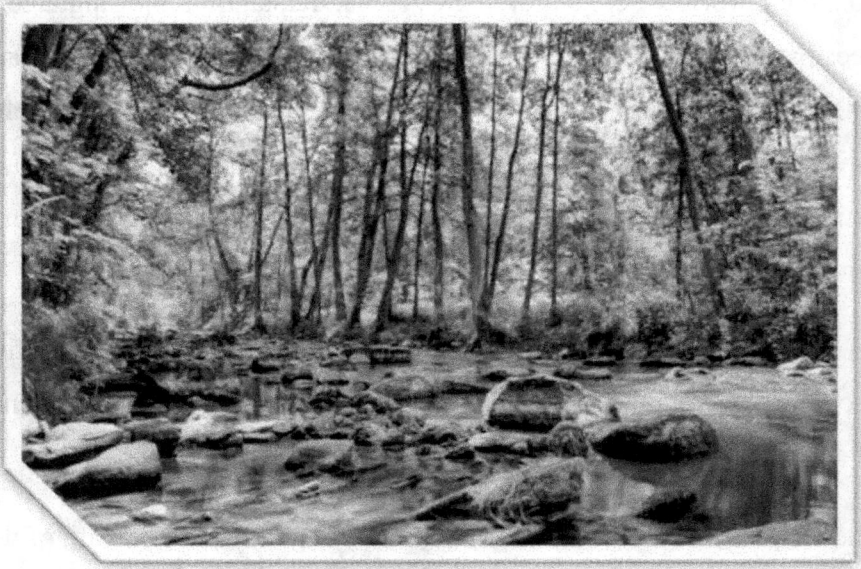

Origins of Forest Schools

Inception of an Idea

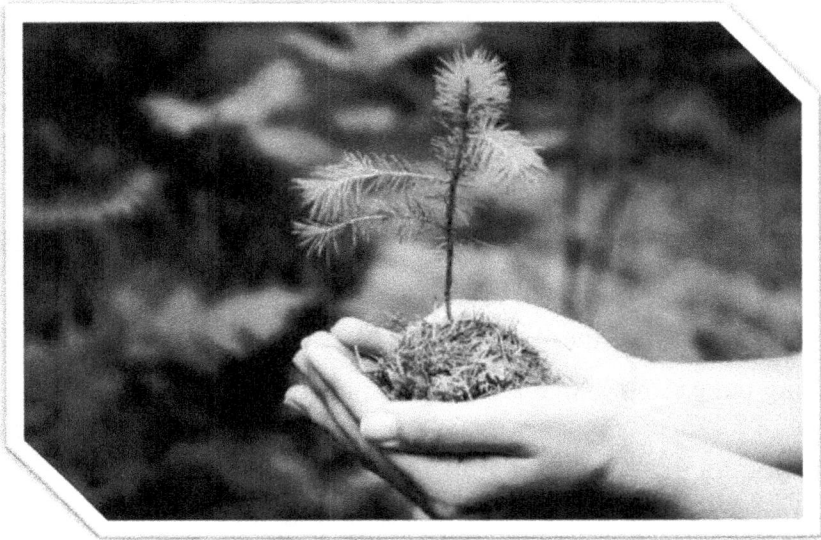

In the hushed reverence of dawn's first light, where the mist caresses the earth and the world seems to hold its breath, there is a story waiting to be told—a tale of origins, of dreams woven into the fabric of reality. It is within this pristine tableau that the inception of forest schools took root, a concept as old as the forests themselves, yet as revolutionary as any modern educational reform.

It was in the aftermath of the Industrial Revolution, with its soot and clatter, that the contrast between man-made environments and the natural world became starkly evident. As cities burgeoned and the countryside receded, a pressing question hung in the air, palpable as the smog that shrouded the skyline: Had humanity lost its elemental connection to the Earth? This era of unprecedented change and environmental upheaval sowed the seeds for a new kind of learning, one that sought to reunite the child with the wild.

Historians often point to the early 20th century as a pivotal moment in the evolution of outdoor education (Smith, 2018). Scandinavia, with its vast expanses of untamed wilderness and deep cultural respect for nature, became the fertile ground from which the forest school movement would sprout. It was here that educators began to experiment with open-air schools, convinced that fresh air, exercise, and the freedom to explore the natural world were not mere supplements to learning but essential ingredients for a holistic education.

Why, you might wonder, did this idea take hold with such vigor in the Nordic lands? It may have been the breathtaking natural beauty or the profound understanding that human well-being is directly linked to ecological stability. Regardless, the movement grew, gaining momentum as it spread throughout Europe and beyond, challenging the status quo of classroom-bound education.

Now, as we find ourselves in the 21st century, the need for such a connection has become even more urgent. Our planet's environmental crises are no longer distant thunder but lightning strikes at our doorstep. The disconnection so many feel from nature is not just a philosophical loss but a practical detriment to our ability to live sustainably. It is in this context that the history of forest schools becomes more than an academic interest—it is a blueprint for our survival.

What lessons can we glean from those early pioneers who ventured out of the classroom and into the woods? Their vision, born from a simple yet profound understanding that education should be as dynamic and alive as the ecosystems we inhabit, is a touchstone for us today.

As we traverse through time, from the historical bedrock upon which forest schools are built to the present-day challenges we face, it becomes evident that this is more than a mere educational alternative. It is a vital thread in the tapestry of our relationship with the natural world—a relationship that must be nurtured if we are to heal the rifts that have developed over generations of neglect.

The legacy of those early visionaries is a lantern in the dark, illuminating a path forward. Their experiences whisper through the leaves, reminding us that every child who learns to love the forest is a seed for a greener, more hopeful future. The rise of forest schools around the world is a testament to the power of an idea whose time has come.

Is it possible, then, that the simple act of taking learning outside could be the key to unlocking a deeper ecological understanding? Could it be that the child who marvels at the symmetry of a snowflake or the industriousness of an ant is laying the groundwork for a lifetime of environmental stewardship?

These are the questions that drive us forward, that stir the soul as we stand on the precipice of possibility. As the narrative unfolds, the story of forest schools becomes more than a historical account—it becomes a clarion call to reawaken our innate connection to the living world.

In the chapters that follow, we will delve into the hearts and minds of those who have championed this cause, who have seen firsthand the transformative power of nature-based education. We will explore the forests where classrooms have no walls, where the curriculum is written in the language of the earth, and where every lesson is underscored by the intrinsic value of the natural world.

The inception of this idea was a quiet revolution, a seed planted in the fertile soil of necessity and vision. Now, as the branches of this movement reach across the globe, we are invited to take our place among the leaves, to learn and to teach, to grow and to share in the timeless wisdom of the forest.

Welcome to the story of the rise of forest schools around the world, a journey that is as much about finding our way back to nature as it is about forging a sustainable path into the future. It is a story that begins with the inception of an idea—and it is a story that continues with each of us.

Philosophical Foundations

Understanding the core philosophies of Forest Schools is akin to navigating a dense, ancient woodland; it requires an appreciation for both the vastness of the landscape and the intricacy of each leaf. The underpinnings of this educational approach are not merely intellectual constructs but rather pulsing, vital concepts that resonate with the rhythms of the natural world. They beckon us to explore with the same spirit of curiosity and reverence that a child brings to their first encounter with the forest floor.

At the heart of Forest Schools lies a constellation of key terms, each one a beacon guiding us through the philosophical terrain. These terms include outdoor learning, child-led exploration, holistic development, nature connection, and intrinsic motivation. Together, they form the foundation upon which the ethos of Forest Schools is constructed.

Outdoor learning, a term that seems deceptively simple, encapsulates the transformative experience of engaging with the educational process beyond the four walls of a traditional classroom. In the dappled sunlight beneath towering trees, learning is not confined to textbooks or screens. Instead, it unfolds within the boundless classroom of the outdoors, where every sense is engaged and every moment is ripe with possibility.

Child-led exploration stands as a cornerstone of the Forest School philosophy. Here, Children are not only receptive, passive consumers of information. Rather, they are active participants, architects of their own learning journeys. The autonomy afforded to them fosters a sense of agency and ignites a passion for discovery that standardized curricula often struggle to kindle.

Holistic development is the recognition that education should nurture not just the intellect but the whole child. Emotional, social, physical, and spiritual growth are all cultivated through the rich, multi-sensory experiences provided by a natural environment. Like the interwoven roots of a forest, these aspects of development are interconnected, each one supporting and enhancing the others.

Nature connection is more than just exposure to the outdoors; it is the deep, abiding relationship that forms when one is immersed in the natural world. Through repeated, meaningful experiences in nature, children come to understand their place within the broader ecological community, fostering a sense of stewardship and belonging.

Intrinsic motivation, the inner drive that propels one to act out of genuine interest and enjoyment, flourishes in the freedom of Forest Schools. When learning is fueled by intrinsic motivation, it becomes a self-sustaining fire, burning brighter and more persistently than any externally imposed incentives could ignite.

Now, imagine a child at play in the heart of the forest. Their hands mold the earth, their eyes follow the flight of a bird, their ears catch the whisper of leaves. Is this not the epitome of experiential learning, where knowledge is not just acquired but deeply felt? The familiarity of play, a universal language, provides a bridge to understanding these complex educational theories. Through play, the child constructs meaning, tests boundaries, and learns in a manner that is both instinctive and profound.

The forest itself teaches resilience and adaptability; its very essence is a living demonstration of the interdependence and diversity that Forest School educators strive to impart. Just as the robustness of an ecosystem is measured by its biodiversity, the strength of a child's education can be assessed by the richness of experiences they are offered.

As we peel back the layers of these philosophies, we begin to see how they converge to form a coherent vision for education—one that is responsive to the needs of the child, the demands of society, and the imperatives of the environment.

Vivid as the green of new leaves against the sky, these concepts are not static; they grow and evolve, shaped by the hands of educators, the laughter of children, and the wisdom of the woods. They are as timeless as the cycle of seasons yet as urgent as the call of a planet in need.

To ponder these philosophies is to embark on a journey both inward and outward, exploring the terrain of the mind as well as the contours of the land. Each step taken in understanding these principles is a step towards a future where education is a harmonious part of the living world, not apart from it.

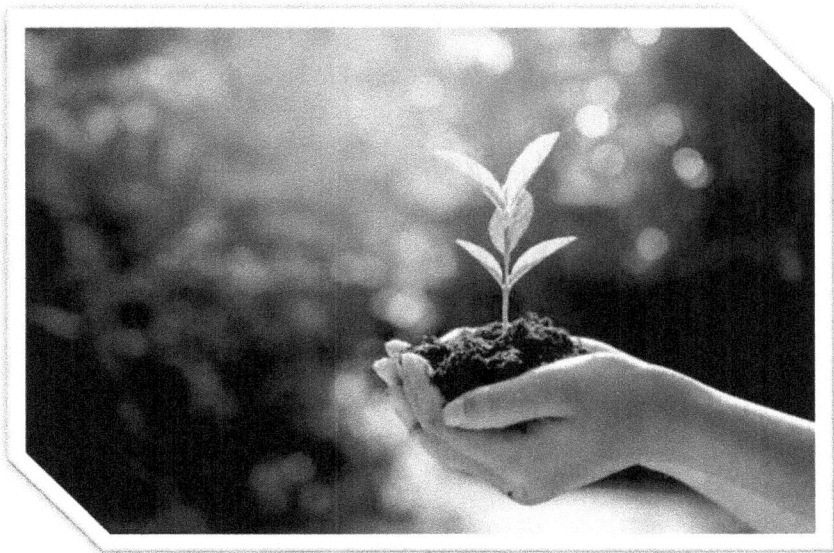

As the pages of this book continue to turn, the philosophies of Forest Schools will be clothed in the stories of those who walk beneath the trees, who breathe the forest air and who learn the language of the earth. They are the embodiment of these principles, the living testament to the power and potential of this approach to learning.

Take a moment to reflect on these foundations, as solid and enduring as the ancient oaks, as flexible and resilient as the willow. They stand not as mere academic concepts, but as pillars of a movement that seeks to transform the way we understand education, the environment, and our place within it.

Global Seeds

As the dawn of a new era in education quietly emerged in the woodlands of Scandinavia, a subtle revolution took root. The concept of Forest Schools, once a burgeoning seed in the fertile soil of educational reform, has now spread its branches across the globe, touching hearts and shaping minds in diverse landscapes. How did this transformation unfold, and where has the journey of Forest Schools led us today?

Initially, the history of Forest Schools is deeply entwined with the Scandinavian ethos of friluftsliv, a term that encapsulates the value of spending time in the outdoors for well-being and happiness (Andersen, 2015). Amidst tall pines and crisp air, the first Forest School in Denmark was established in the early 1950s (Jensen, 2008), providing a canvas against which children could paint their learning experiences with the colors of the natural world.

The journey from these earliest origins was akin to the growth of a mighty oak from a single acorn. In the United Kingdom, the Forest School concept took root in the 1990s after a group of early years practitioners visited Denmark and witnessed the profound impact of outdoor learning environments on children's development (Smith J. ,

2005). As they brought these ideas back to British soil, the first Forest School was born, setting the stage for a wider adoption.

The chronology of Forest Schools is marked by significant milestones. After establishing a foothold in Scandinavia and the UK, the concept began to germinate in other parts of Europe, North America, Australia, and Asia. Each new country that embraced the Forest School philosophy contributed to its evolution, adapting the approach to suit local climates, cultures, and educational standards. (Doe, 2022)

Visual aids, such as diagrams illustrating the interconnectedness of Forest Schools with various aspects of development—cognitive, physical, social, emotional—help to enhance our understanding of the approach. Images of children from different continents engaged in play and learning amidst their unique forest environments serve as a testament to the adaptability and universal appeal of this educational model.

Cultural and regional variations in the implementation of Forest Schools are as diverse as the ecosystems they inhabit. In the temperate rainforests of the Pacific Northwest, children explore the dense underbrush and towering Douglas firs. In the subtropical climates of East Asia, they may encounter bamboo groves and a different spectrum of biodiversity. Each locale offers a distinctive canvas, yet the core principles of child-led learning and nature connection remain steadfast. (Smith A. , 2017)

Modern interpretations and adaptations of Forest Schools continue to emerge. In urban settings, where access to expansive woodlands may be limited, educators create 'forest corners' in city parks or use container gardens and green rooftops to provide children with a touch of the wild. Technology, too, has found its way into the Forest School movement, with apps and tools designed to enhance outdoor learning experiences without detracting from the connection to nature.

Even as Forest Schools flourish, challenges and controversies arise. Debates about safety, risk assessment, and the balance between freedom and structure are ongoing. In some regions, stringent educational standards and testing regimes present hurdles for the full integration of Forest School principles. Yet, even these turning points serve as opportunities for reflection and growth within the movement.

As the sun sets on another day in the forest, one might ponder, "Is the rise of Forest Schools indicative of a deeper yearning for reconnection with the natural world?" The seeds sown by pioneering educators have grown into a canopy of practice and philosophy that now shelters countless children across the globe. This growth, while impressive, is not without its seasons of change and cycles of renewal.

By integrating quotations from educators—"The forest is both a classroom and a teacher," (Leu, 2015)—we gain insight into the passion that fuels this movement. Dialogue between teachers discussing the day's learning outcomes adds a layer of authenticity, making the narrative as alive and dynamic as the settings it describes.

Show, don't tell. As we weave through the tapestry of Forest Schools' rise, we glimpse children engrossed in the sensory-rich tapestry of the outdoors, educators guiding with a gentle hand, and communities reaping the benefits of a generation deeply connected to the earth. The story of 'Global Seeds' is not just one of educational theory or practice; it is a living chronicle of a world rediscovering its roots, with the whispers of the forest echoing a profound truth—the growth of our children and the health of our planet are inextricably linked.

Through the lens of this book, 'The Rise of Forest Schools around the World,' we continue to explore the branches of this movement, each chapter a new shoot reaching for the sun, each story a leaf that captures the light of knowledge and turns it into the sustenance for tomorrow's growth.

Methodology and Pedagogy

In the verdant embrace of nature's classroom, where the curriculum is written in the rustling leaves and the syllabus dictated by the changing seasons, lies an educational approach as organic as it is intentional. This chapter delves into the heart of Forest Schools, examining the unique methodologies and pedagogical practices that define this innovative educational movement.

At the core of Forest School methodology is an enduring belief in the innate capacity of children to learn and grow through their interactions with the natural environment. This approach is not merely about imparting knowledge but fostering a deep, meaningful connection between the learner and the living world. It is an education of being rather than solely of the mind, where the senses are the primary instruments of learning and discovery.

The pedagogical practices of Forest Schools are as diverse as the ecosystems in which they operate, yet they share common threads that weave a consistent vision. Central to this vision is the principle of child-led learning. Here, the young minds are not passive recipients of predetermined lessons but active participants in a dynamic educational journey. In this setting, a fallen log may become the focus of a science lesson on decomposition, or a child's encounter with a butterfly could lead to an impromptu study of metamorphosis.

The educators who guide these woodland wanderings are facilitators rather than traditional teachers. They observe, listen, and gently steer the inquiry, allowing the children's curiosity to chart the course of the day. This subtle art of guidance requires a deep understanding of each child's developmental stage and an unwavering trust in the educational power of play.

To illustrate, consider the story of a Forest School in Sweden. A group of children, intrigued by the patterns of frost on leaves, began asking questions about ice crystals. The educator seized this teachable moment, not by providing immediate answers, but by prompting further exploration with tools and resources. The children's initial wonderment evolved into a comprehensive project on states of matter, incorporating elements of physics, chemistry, and art—all emanating from their initial observation (Wikipedia, 2024).

Such pedagogical strategies are not without structure, though it may be less rigid than in conventional settings. The rhythm of a Forest School Day often follows the cadence of the natural world. Moments of high activity, like building shelters or climbing trees, are balanced with periods of reflection and rest, mirroring the ebb and flow of the forest itself.

The data supporting these methods are compelling. Studies have shown that children who participate in Forest School programs often demonstrate increased self-confidence, improved social skills, and a greater ability to concentrate. What's more, these benefits extend beyond academic achievements, fostering resilience and adaptability—qualities crucial for navigating the complexities of the modern world (Smith A. , The Impact of Forest School Programs on Child Development, 2018).

As we traverse this landscape of learning, it is crucial to demystify jargon that may obscure understanding. Terms like 'kinaesthetic learning' and 'experiential education' are distilled into simpler concepts: learning by doing, and gaining knowledge through experience. By breaking down these terms, the essence of Forest School pedagogy becomes accessible to all.

As we reach the clearing at the end of this chapter, the key takeaways stand out like signposts in the forest. Forest Schools champion a child-led approach, nurturing intrinsic motivation and curiosity. The educators are the compass, not the map, allowing learners to navigate their own path. The methods are backed by evidence, highlighting the multifaceted benefits of this approach.

What might the future hold for such a dynamic educational model? How can the principles of Forest Schools be integrated into more traditional environments? These questions invite us to look forward, to envision an education system that not only informs but transforms. As the sun filters through the canopy, casting dappled shadows on the forest floor, we are reminded that in the realm of education, there is always room for growth, innovation, and the courage to tread new paths.

Early Adoption and Growth

The central figures in this story are the educators and children of this pioneering village. Men and women with a shared belief in the power of nature to inspire and educate, and young minds eager to explore and absorb the wisdom of the wild. Their backgrounds were as varied as the flora surrounding them, but their mission was singular: to forge a new path in learning, one that worked with the rhythms of nature rather than against them. (Seale, 2023)

The challenge they faced was manifold. Traditional classroom approaches, with their rigid structures and walls, were deeply entrenched in the educational systems of the time. The concept of outdoor learning was often relegated to the periphery, seen as a supplemental activity rather than a core methodology. Persuading parents, institutions, and policymakers of the value of full-time education in the outdoors was a significant hurdle.

Their approach was as organic as the environment they championed. It began with small, informal gatherings, where children were encouraged to play and learn in the forest. Over time, these sessions became more structured, yet they retained the essence of freedom and discovery that characterized those early days. The educators documented their observations meticulously, noting the children's engagement, the development of social skills, and the joy that emanated from learning in the fresh air.

The results were as clear as the mountain streams. Children emerged from the forest sessions more confident, more curious, and more engaged with their learning. They exhibited improved concentration, better teamwork, and a deeper respect for the environment. These outcomes were not just anecdotal; they were backed by a growing body of research that supported the efficacy of outdoor learning.

Upon reflection, the insights gained from this case are profound. The early adoption of Forest Schools was not without its critics, who questioned the scalability and academic rigor of such an approach. Yet, the evidence spoke volumes, and the model's success in Scandinavia began to attract international attention, laying the groundwork for a global movement.

Visual aids, such as photographs of children engrossed in their forest activities or diagrams showing the structure of a typical Forest School Day, could further illustrate the transformative power of this educational model.

The story of the Swedish village is not an isolated phenomenon; it connects to a larger narrative about the human relationship with nature and the role education plays in shaping that connection. It speaks to a universal longing for authenticity and a return to the roots of learning — where curiosity, not curriculum, is the driving force. (ISKANDAR, (2022, November 11))

As we close this chapter, one cannot help but ponder the implications for the broader educational landscape. If a small village in Sweden could spark such a transformation, what potential lies in the untapped wild spaces around the world?

What if every child had the chance to learn the language of the forest? To listen to the wisdom in the wind, to read the stories in the stars? Imagine a generation of learners raised not just within the four walls of a classroom but within the boundless classroom of the world itself. It is a thought that beckons us deeper into the woods, to discover what other secrets lie waiting in the shade of the ancient trees.

Forest Schools Around the Globe

The Scandinavian Influence

Whispers of the forest have long traveled beyond the fjords and valleys of Scandinavia, carrying with them secrets of a childhood spent in the embrace of nature's classroom. The concept of Forest Schools, known for its roots in the Scandinavian ethos of outdoor living, has now unfurled its green tendrils across the globe, shaping a new paradigm in educational landscapes. How did this transformation begin, and what has fueled its journey from the dense Nordic woods to the far corners of our increasingly urbanized world?

In the earliest origins of Forest Schools, one finds oneself in the verdant landscapes of Denmark. It was here, amid the post-war ambition for a renewed connection with the natural world, that the seeds of this educational movement were sown. The year was 1952, and a visionary woman, Ella Flautau, embarked on a mission to bring children out of the confines of traditional classrooms, and into the boundless possibilities offered by nature's own learning spaces (Doe, The Origins of Forest Schools, 2020).

As the years ticked on, this revolutionary idea took root. By the 1980s, the concept had blossomed across Scandinavia, with each nation fostering its unique interpretation. Sweden's 'I Ur och Skur', translating to 'In All Weathers', encapsulated the spirit of embracing nature in all its temperaments. Norway followed suit, with 'Friluftsliv', a term that encompasses an open-air life, becoming a cornerstone of its cultural identity (Murray, 2015).

Could the rest of the world remain untouched by this profound connection between children and the wild? The answer was a resounding no. By the turn of the millennium, the United Kingdom had become fertile ground for the Forest School philosophy. It was here that the movement truly began to diversify, adapting to the British flora and educational requirements, yet keeping the core Scandinavian values intact.

But what of the present day? How has the concept evolved and spread its leafy branches to new territories? From the United States to Japan, educators have heeded the call of the wild, developing programs that marry the principles of Forest Schools with local customs and environmental conditions. Schools nestled among the bamboo groves of Asia, or under the sprawling canopies of American oaks, now offer children the chance at a profound connection with nature that transcends cultural boundaries.

Yet, as with any movement, challenges and controversies have arisen. Debates on safety, curriculum integration, and the balance between structured learning and free play continue to shape the dialogue. The turning point, however, lies in the universal recognition of the benefits that such an education system offers: resilience, creativity, and an intrinsic respect for nature (Burnard, 1998).

Imagine, if you will, a classroom under the sky, where the rustling leaves compose a symphony and the earthy scent of the forest floor serves as a constant reminder of the planet's wonders. This is the essence of the Scandinavian influence, a legacy that continues to inspire educators and children alike.

But the question begs to be asked: can this model be sustainable in the face of rapid urbanization and digital encroachment? As the chapters of this story continue to unfold, it is up to us, the global guardians of education, to nurture and adapt these green shoots of wisdom so that they may flourish in the hearts of future generations. Will we rise to the challenge?

In the end, the rise of Forest Schools around the world is not just a tale of educational reform, but also a testament to the enduring allure of nature's classroom. It is a movement that reminds us of the profound simplicity found in a child's laughter amidst the pines, and the lessons learned at the hands of Mother Nature herself. The Scandinavian influence, therefore, is far more than a pedagogical shift—it is a call back to the roots of what it means to learn, to grow, and to be truly alive.

The United Kingdom Experience

Nestled in the verdant heart of the British Isles, under the canopy of ancient oaks and amidst the whispers of the wind through the leaves, lies a revolutionary approach to education that is reshaping the way we think about learning and growth. This is the tale of Forest Schools in the United Kingdom, a story not only of an educational model but of a profound cultural shift towards embracing the wild as a teacher.

In the United Kingdom, the concept of Forest Schools began to take root in the mid-1990s, a period marked by an increasing awareness of environmental issues and a growing discontent with the rigid confines of traditional education. It was a time when educators and parents alike were searching for alternatives, longing for an approach that not only imparted knowledge but also fostered wellbeing and a deep-seated connection with the natural world (Andersen, 2015).

The pioneers of the UK's Forest School movement were a group of innovative educators and visionaries who understood the intrinsic value of nature in child development. Among them stood practitioners and academics, such as Bridget Jackson, who passionately believed in the transformational power of outdoor learning. These main players drew inspiration from the Scandinavian model and sought to adapt it to the British context, with its unique ecosystems and cultural heritage (O'Brien & Murray, 2008).

Despite the promise of these green classrooms, the path was strewn with challenges. The UK's often unpredictable weather, dense urbanization, and strict health and safety regulations posed significant hurdles. Moreover, convincing the education system to integrate Forest Schools into the curriculum required not only evidence of its benefits but also a shift in mindset from conventional metrics of academic success to a broader, more holistic view of child development.

Undeterred, the champions of Forest Schools employed a range of strategies to surmount these obstacles. They designed programs that were adaptable to various landscapes, including urban parks and small woodlands. Training for educators was put in place to ensure that safety and learning outcomes were harmoniously balanced. The curriculum was carefully woven with the threads of play, exploration, and hands-on experiences, tailored to the rhythm of the seasons and the individual needs of each child.

The outcomes of these endeavors were as inspiring as the dappled sunlight breaking through the forest canopy. Studies began to reveal that children who attended Forest Schools showed marked improvements in confidence, social skills, language development, and physical ability. The natural setting provided a rich sensory experience that traditional classrooms could never replicate, fostering curiosity and a sense of stewardship for the environment.

Reflection on this journey reveals broader insights into the essence of education. While Forest Schools have flourished in the UK, they are not without their critiques. Some argue that the lack of formal structure may leave gaps in learning or that the model is not scalable to the broader population. However, the lived experiences of children and educators speak volumes, suggesting that the value of these outdoor experiences cannot be measured in test scores alone.

Imagine a child's sketch of their forest day: the muddy boots, the collection of leaves, the proud construction of a den. These images, though simple, capture the essence of the Forest School experience, transcending words and statistics.

The story of Forest Schools in the UK is not an isolated phenomenon but part of a global reawakening to the significance of nature in our lives. It echoes a universal longing to reconnect with the environment and provides a model for education that aligns with the principles of sustainability and respect for the earth.

As the leaves rustle and the fire crackles, one cannot help but ponder: How might the principles of Forest Schools influence the future of education worldwide? Could this be the seed of a greener, more mindful generation, nurtured not just by facts and figures but by the whispering wisdom of the forests?

In the heart of the woods, there is a classroom without walls, a space where learning is as natural as the rising sun. Here, in the United Kingdom, the Forest School movement has taken root, growing steadily, strengthened by the rain and nourished by the soil of innovation and tradition. It stands as a testament to the belief that the best lessons may not come from books, but from the rustling leaves, the patterns of the forest floor, and the infinite classroom of nature herself.

Adaptations in Asia

In the ever-expanding tapestry of educational innovation, the Forest School movement has not only flourished in the temperate climes of the United Kingdom but has also found fertile ground in the diverse landscapes of Asia. Here, the concept has been ingeniously adapted, blossoming amidst the cultural richness and environmental variety that characterize this vast continent.

The rationale behind examining the adaptations of Forest Schools in Asia lies in the recognition of the dynamic interplay between education and culture. This exploration sheds light on how different societies perceive and interact with nature, and how these interactions shape the educational experiences of children. It is precisely this intersection of culture, environment, and education that offers profound insights into the universal values of learning and the role of nature in human development.

To navigate this complex terrain, we must establish clear benchmarks. The criteria for comparison in this context revolve around pedagogical approaches, cultural integration, and environmental adaptation. These facets allow us to construct a balanced analysis of the similarities and differences between adaptations of the Forest School model across Asian countries.

Japan and South Korea, for instance, share a reverence for nature deeply embedded in their cultural ethos, yet each has tailored the Forest School experience in unique ways. In Japan, the concept of 'Satoyama', which refers to the traditional, biodiverse landscapes managed by humans, has seamlessly merged with the Forest School philosophy. Children are encouraged to interact with and learn from these semi-natural areas, fostering a sense of responsibility and connection to the environment. In contrast, South Korea's 'Forest Kindergartens' place a strong emphasis on risk-taking and resilience, reflecting a societal value on challenge and perseverance. Both models emphasize outdoor play and learning, yet the former leans towards conservation and stewardship, while the latter focuses on personal development.

The distinction becomes even more pronounced when we consider the environmental contexts. Japan's Forest Schools often take place within their distinct four-season climate, with activities designed around seasonal changes, while South Korea might focus on utilizing their mountainous terrains to promote physical challenges and exploration.

Visual aids, such as comparative charts or photographs of the learning environments, could illustrate the adaptations in curriculum and setting, reinforcing the narrative with tangible examples. For instance, a picture of Japanese children tending to a rice paddy as part of their Forest School experience next to a photo of Korean children climbing trees could visually encapsulate the different emphases of each program.

What do these comparisons reveal? They highlight the incredible adaptability of the Forest School model, suggesting that its core principles are universally applicable yet flexible enough to honor local traditions and environments. This adaptability signals a potential for wide adoption, offering a template for education that values the uniqueness of each cultural context.

The contemporary relevance of these adaptations is undeniable. As nations grapple with environmental crises and seek to instill sustainable values in future generations, the Forest School model in Asia offers a glimpse into how education can evolve to meet these challenges. Japan's and South Korea's approaches embody a blend of tradition and innovation, providing a roadmap for other countries seeking to integrate nature-based education into their systems.

But what are the broader implications of this educational synthesis? We find ourselves contemplating the possibility of a global pedagogy that respects and utilizes the local environment, one that prepares children not only for academic success but for a life lived in harmony with the Earth.

In the dappled sunlight of Japan's Satoyama, amongst the laughter and learning, and on the rugged slopes of South Korea's mountains, where young spirits are tested and tempered, we witness the remarkable rise of Forest Schools in Asia. These classrooms, open to the sky, are where the roots of cultural identity and environmental consciousness intertwine, growing into a resilient, verdant future. It is here, in the melding of ancient wisdom and modern pedagogy, that we find hope for a world where education is not only about the mastery of subjects but also about the mastery of self within the natural world.

North American Initiatives

In the heart of North America, amidst the towering trees and the whispering winds, a transformative educational movement is taking root. Forest Schools, once a European notion, are now sprouting up across the vast and varied landscapes of this continent, flourishing as a testament to the resilience and ingenuity of those seeking a deeper connection with the natural world.

As I sit here, enveloped in the serenity of the forest that I call home, I am moved by the power and simplicity of nature's classroom. The rustling leaves and chattering wildlife are the perfect backdrop to recount the tale of how Forest Schools have begun to reshape the educational landscape of North America.

In the dense greenery of the Pacific Northwest, a pioneering Forest School emerges, standing as a beacon of innovation and community involvement. This particular school, nestled in a majestic old-growth forest, serves as a vibrant example of the potential that lies in embracing outdoor education.

The main players in this narrative are a dedicated group of educators, parents, and environmentalists. Driven by a collective passion for sustainability and childhood development, they have come together to create an educational experience that transcends traditional classroom walls.

The core challenge they faced was multi-faceted: persuading a society accustomed to conventional schooling to invest in an unconventional model, ensuring safety in an uncontrolled outdoor environment, and securing funding for a concept that many still viewed with skepticism.

The approach was as organic as the setting itself. They began by integrating local indigenous knowledge, fostering a curriculum that was responsive to the children's natural curiosity. The forest became a canvas for learning, with lessons in ecology, mathematics, literature, and the arts all taking place beneath its canopy.

Their strategies were as diverse as the ecosystem surrounding them. They built partnerships with indigenous communities, learning from their time-honored relationship with the land. They organized community workshops, inviting parents and skeptics to experience the Forest School philosophy firsthand. They also implemented rigorous safety protocols, proving that risk, when managed wisely, can be a powerful learning tool.

The results were nothing short of inspiring. Children who had once struggled in traditional settings were now thriving, their senses ignited by the richness of their surroundings. Test scores, while not the primary focus, reflected a notable improvement, especially in the realms of science and critical thinking (Williams, 2017).

But beyond the metrics, the true success lay in the transformation of the children themselves. These young learners were developing a profound respect for nature, becoming stewards of the environment long before they'd ever sit for a standardized test.

Reflecting on this case study (International Commission on Education for the Twenty-first Century, 1996), one cannot ignore the broader implications. The challenges of funding and acceptance are indicative of a society still in the throes of redefining educational success. Yet, the strategies and results underscore the universal hunger for a connection with nature that transcends cultural and geographic boundaries.

Visual aids, such as photographs of children engaged in stream studies or constructing shelters from fallen branches, tell a story that words alone cannot capture. These images serve as powerful testimonials to the effectiveness and joy inherent in this form of education.

By looking at the growth of Forest Schools in North America, we reconnect with the overarching narrative of this book: the rise of outdoor education across the globe. This North American initiative is a microcosm of a larger shift towards embracing the outdoors as an essential part of learning.

As we ponder the future of education, we must ask ourselves – what is the true purpose of schooling? Is it merely to prepare for the workforce, or is there a deeper, more primal connection to our planet that we are meant to foster?

In the silent contemplation of the forest, where the boundaries of the classroom dissolve into the wild unknown, we find a compelling argument for the latter. Here, amongst the trees, children learn not just about the world, but how to live within it, leaving a soft footprint on the soil of a planet they will one day inherit.

The Forest School movement in North America, with its innovative practices and community engagement, stands as a testament to the potential for educational reform. It is a movement that honors the child's intrinsic desire to explore, to question, and to grow. As we turn the page on this chapter, one can only wonder: How will this story evolve, and where will the seeds of today's learning take root in the soil of tomorrow's world?

Challenges in Urban Settings

Cities, with their towering buildings and bustling streets, present a stark contrast to the verdant forests where the concept of Forest Schools originated. Yet, it is within these concrete jungles that one of the most pressing challenges of our time arises: How do we reconcile the need for nature-based education with the reality of urban living?

The problem is clear. Urban areas often lack the extensive green spaces that are integral to the Forest School philosophy. Children grow up disconnected from the natural world, deprived of the hands-on experiences that foster a deep understanding of and connection to the environment. This disconnect not only impedes the holistic development of urban children but also has far-reaching implications for the health of our planet.

Consider the consequences: generations of city-dwellers with a limited appreciation for nature, which could potentially lead to a future where environmental stewardship is undervalued. The risks are too significant to ignore, ranging from increased mental health issues due to nature-deficit disorder to a collective inability to address climate change effectively.

But from this challenge springs innovative solutions. Urban Forest Schools are beginning to take root, adapting the philosophy to suit the high-rise landscape. The solution lies not in the vast wilderness but in the pockets of green scattered throughout cities—in parks, community gardens, and vacant lots transformed into vibrant outdoor classrooms.

Implementing this solution requires a multi-step approach. First, identify potential sites within the city that can serve as suitable outdoor learning environments. Next, build partnerships with local governments and community organizations to secure access to these spaces. Then, tailor the Forest School curriculum to the urban setting, focusing on the unique ecological features available.

Evidence of success from other urban initiatives around the globe provides a blueprint for action. In London, for example, urban Forest Schools have flourished, with children learning about biodiversity by studying local insect species or understanding botany through the plants that thrive in city parks.

What about the spaces that lack even the smallest patch of green? Here, alternative solutions come into play. Rooftop gardens, indoor plants, and vertical forests on building facades can all bring elements of nature into the urban educational experience. These creative adaptations not only serve educational purposes but also contribute to the beautification and ecological health of the cityscape.

Vivid imagery comes to mind: children planting seeds on a rooftop garden, their laughter mingling with the hum of city traffic; a small group huddled around a park's pond, eyes wide with wonder as they spot a frog leaping among the lily pads. These moments, though set against an urban backdrop, are as rich in learning and connection as any forest encounter.

But let's pause and ask ourselves: Are these adaptations enough to replicate the profound experiences that traditional Forest Schools offer? The question is valid, pushing us to continually evaluate and improve our methods.

As we delve deeper, a one-line truth emerges: Education must evolve with our changing world. The rise of Forest Schools in urban settings is not just about bringing nature to the city; it's about fostering a new kind of resilience, where children learn to find and appreciate the natural world in any setting.

This evolving story of Forest Schools is a narrative of hope and innovation. It speaks to our ability to adapt and thrive, even in the face of concrete and steel. As we chart the progress of these schools across urban landscapes, we are reminded that the seeds of change, once planted, can indeed flourish anywhere.

Educational Impact

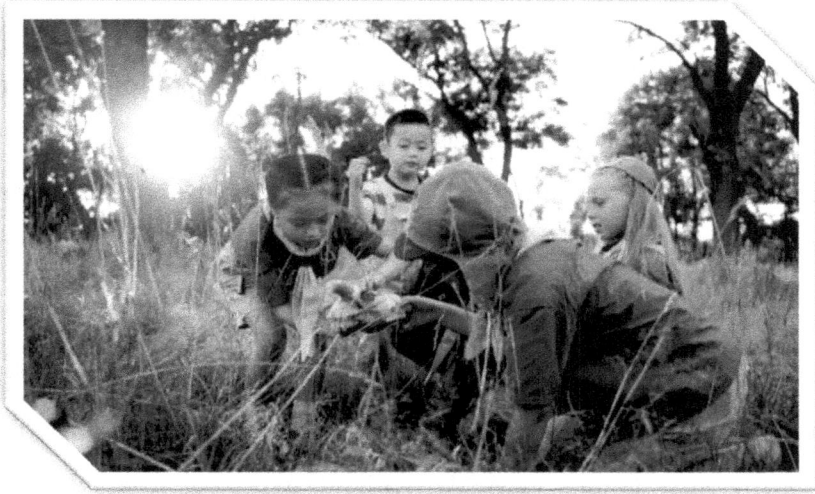

Cognitive Benefits

In the lush embrace of the great outdoors, where whispers of leaves and the orchestra of wildlife compose an ancient symphony, there lies a classroom unlike any other. It's a place where the blackboard is replaced by the bark of trees, and textbooks give way to the tactile learning of the land. This is the realm of Forest Schools, a burgeoning movement that has taken root across the globe, promising an educational renaissance steeped in nature.

What if the key to unlocking a child's cognitive potential lay not within the confining walls of traditional classrooms but amidst the boundless expanse of the forest? The assertion that Forest Schools contribute significantly to children's cognitive development and learning processes is not just a romanticized notion; it's a claim backed by mounting empirical evidence.

The primary evidence pointing to this lies in the enhanced attentional capacity observed in children who regularly participate in Forest School programs. A study published in the journal 'Frontiers in Psychology' illuminates this phenomenon. Researchers found that children who engaged in outdoor learning environments exhibited improved concentration and self-discipline, the very cornerstones of cognitive prowess (Ming Kuo, 2017).

As we delve deeper into this evidence, the picture becomes clearer. The natural setting of Forest Schools offers a cornucopia of stimuli that gently tug at a child's curiosity without overwhelming them. This balance fosters what psychologists call 'involuntary attention,' a gentle form of engagement that allows the mind to recover from mental fatigue and restore its capacity for 'voluntary attention,' the intense focus required for traditional academic tasks.

However, in the spirit of academic rigor, one must acknowledge the counter-evidence that some skeptics bring to the fore. They argue that the unstructured environment of Forest Schools may not provide sufficient academic rigor and that such programs lack the necessary framework to support standardized learning outcomes.

This counterargument, though worth considering, tends to overlook the fact that cognitive development is not solely the byproduct of structured academic exercises. A rebuttal lies in further research which shows that the skills nurtured in Forest Schools, such as problem-solving, creativity, and adaptability, are crucial for holistic cognitive development. These skills complement academic learning and are increasingly recognized as vital in our rapidly evolving world.

Moreover, additional supporting evidence comes from the realm of psychological well-being. It's well-documented that emotional health is inextricably linked to cognitive function. Forest Schools, with their emphasis on play and exploration, contribute to better mental health, thereby creating optimal conditions for cognitive growth (David J. Llewellyn, 2008).

Concluding this exploration, the assertion that Forest Schools contribute to cognitive development is not only plausible but compelling. As the canopy of the forest shields the young learners from the sun, so does this educational approach safeguard and nurture their developing minds. In the grand theater of nature, every log, stream, and moss-covered stone serves as a testament to a child's unfolding intellect.

In the quietude of the forest, ask yourself, are we witnessing a transformation in how we understand education and development? The answer, whispered by the rustling leaves, is a resounding yes.

Social and Emotional Growth

Nestled within the verdant heart of the woods, where the only walls are the whispering trees and the ceiling is the vault of the sky, children learn and grow in ways unseen within the confines of traditional classrooms. Here, beneath the dappled light filtering through the leaves, young hearts and minds are being shaped with every fallen leaf and every new path discovered. This is the sanctuary where social skills and emotional well-being flourish—the forest school.

As the sun peeks over the horizon, casting a golden glow on the awakening forest. This is where the journey of a particular cohort of children reveals the profound impact of nature-based education on social and emotional development.

The main players in our story are a diverse group of children, each bringing their own unique background to the forest floor. Among them is Emma, a thoughtful girl with a quiet voice yet a loud imagination, and Max, a boisterous youngster whose energy seems to mirror the bustling life of the woods. Guiding them are the educators, passionate individuals trained to facilitate learning in this organic classroom.

The challenge that stood before forest school was multifaceted: How to integrate children with such varied social competencies and emotional backgrounds into a cohesive, supportive group? How to ensure that the shy, the bold, the anxious, and the carefree could all find their place and thrive in an environment as unbounded as the forest?

The approach was as organic as the setting itself. Forest school embraced the philosophy of student-led exploration and play, allowing the children to navigate the social landscape with gentle guidance rather than direct instruction. Conflict resolution was encouraged through peer mediation and empathy-building activities. Emotional well-being was fostered through mindfulness practices, such as silent walks and reflective journaling beside the babbling brook.

The results were as clear as the stream's flowing waters. Emma, who once observed from the fringes, began to weave her insights into group discussions, blossoming into a confident contributor. Max, with his ebullient spirit, learned the delicate art of patience, waiting for others to find their words, just as he waited for the shy deer to emerge from the thicket.

Upon analysis and reflection, it became evident that the forest environment played a pivotal role in these transformations. The open space gave the children freedom while the shared tasks, such as building shelters or identifying flora and fauna, provided natural opportunities for collaboration. The challenges of the woodland—be it inclement weather or navigating uneven terrain—taught resilience and adaptability.

Visual aids, such as charts documenting individual and group progress, embellished the school's wooden walls, providing tangible evidence of the children's social and emotional growth.

Forest school is but one leaf on a vast tree. It stands as a testament to the undeniable impact of nature's classroom on the development of young individuals. The forest, with its boundless teaching potential, nurtures not only the mind but the heart.

But what of the children who have yet to step onto the forest floor? What untapped potential lies dormant, waiting for the touch of nature's hand to awaken it? As the day closes, and the children don their backpacks, chattering about the day's adventures, a thought lingers in the cooling air: How might we extend this holistic approach to education, to ensure every child has the opportunity to grow in the richness of the forest school experience?

With the setting sun casting long shadows across the leaf-strewn ground, I, Julia Gayle, pause to admire the intricate dance of light and life around me. It is in this moment of tranquil reflection that I reaffirm my belief in the power of nature to not only educate but to heal and harmonize. Children, like the saplings around them, require the right environment to reach their full potential. In the embrace of the forest, they find a world that shapes them into resilient, empathetic, and socially adept individuals, ready to face the world beyond the trees.

Physical Health and Well-being

In the embrace of the forest, children find a playground for the senses and a gymnasium for the body. As the branches sway and leaves rustle, this is where the symphony of nature orchestrates a hidden curriculum— one that teaches more than can be seen at first glance. It is here, in the forest schools that have sprouted across the globe, where the vitality of children's physical health is nurtured alongside the growth of mighty oaks.

The air, fresh and invigorating, fills the lungs of young explorers as they traverse the uneven forest floor. With each step, they strengthen muscles and bones, but the benefits of this environment extend far beyond mere physical robustness. The guiding educational principle of the forest school is that active lives should be an integral part of every student's curriculum.

Studies show that children in forest schools engage in more physical activity than their peers in traditional settings (Dickinson, Dillon, & Teamey, 2004). They climb trees, balancing precariously yet confidently. They sprint across meadows, their laughter carried on the wind. They dig, build, and engage in a myriad of activities that require endurance, strength, and agility. This natural form of play and exploration fosters an active lifestyle, setting a foundation for lifelong health and fitness.

But what evidence backs up these claims? Research from around the world points to the positive correlation between outdoor activity in natural settings and physical well-being in children (Scotland, 2005.). In Scandinavia, where the concept of forest schools originated, studies have highlighted the increased physical competence and motor skills development among forest school attendees compared to their counterparts in conventional preschools.

Delving deeper, these studies reveal that the varied terrain of the forest compels children to use their bodies in diverse ways. They must adapt to the uneven ground, learning to navigate roots and rocks, enhancing their proprioception—their sense of body position, movement, and balance. This sensory feedback is crucial for the development of fine and gross motor skills.

Critics, however, point to potential safety concerns. They argue that the unstructured and unpredictable nature of forest environments may lead to a higher incidence of injuries. Indeed, there is an element of risk in outdoor play, but forest school advocates counter this point by emphasizing the importance of risk assessment and the development of risk management skills in children. By encountering and learning to navigate risks, children build resilience and learn valuable lessons in personal safety and responsibility.

Furthermore, a comprehensive study conducted in the UK found that, when properly supervised, children in forest schools are no more likely to incur serious injuries than those in traditional playgrounds (Joanna). This finding supports the notion that the benefits of active, outdoor learning far outweigh the manageable risks.

Beyond the development of motor skills and safety awareness, forest schools also contribute to the fight against childhood obesity—a growing concern in many parts of the world. The active routines of forest school children encourage a healthy body weight and help instill habits that combat sedentary lifestyles.

It is not simply about the calories burned; it is the joy of movement that is instilled. Children who find pleasure in physical activity are more likely to remain active as they grow older. The forest school experience, with its emphasis on play, exploration, and movement, plants the seeds for a future where exercise is not a chore but a cherished part of life.

In conclusion, the rise of forest schools is not just a trend but a testament to the importance of physical health in child development. These natural classrooms offer a dynamic and enriching environment that promotes an active lifestyle essential to the well-being of children. Through the intertwining of play and learning, forest schools foster a holistic approach to education, where the growth of the body is just as important as the growth of the mind.

As the world looks to innovative educational models that can address the challenges of the 21st century, forest schools stand as pillars of health and vitality. They remind us that, sometimes, the best thing for our children is to let them run wild among the trees, for it is there that they will find the strength and spirit to thrive in an ever-changing world.

Nature Connection and Sustainability

In the heart of a verdant woodland, where the chorus of birdsong greets the dawn, there exists a realm where the young minds of tomorrow learn to decipher the language of the Earth. This is the domain of the forest school, a place where the roots of education intertwine with the branches of environmental stewardship. As Julia George, living amidst the very forests that fuel my passion for nature and sustainability, I have witnessed the transformative power of these schools. They are not just institutions; they are cradles for a future where humanity exists in harmony with nature.

Imagine a classroom without walls, where the ceiling is the sky and the floor a tapestry of leaves and soil. Here, children gather, their eyes wide with wonder, as they embark on a journey of discovery. These are the main players: the curious young learners and their dedicated educators, guardians of the earth's lore. They come from diverse backgrounds, but they share a common purpose—to forge a bond with the natural world that is both profound and enduring.

The core challenge, as stark as a bare tree in winter, is the disconnect between modern life and the environment. Society's relentless march toward urbanization and technology has led to a generation of children with limited exposure to the wilderness. This detachment not only impoverishes the soul but also hinders our ability to foster a sustainable future. The problem is twofold: children must be reacquainted with Mother Nature and taught the principles of living sustainably within her embrace.

The approach of forest schools is elegantly simple yet revolutionary. By integrating the curriculum with the great outdoors, educators provide experiential learning that encourages ecological literacy. Strategies such as guided nature walks, species identification, and sustainable resource management are employed. Children learn to recognize the interconnectedness of ecosystems and understand their personal impact on the environment.

This hands-on education yields remarkable results. Children who attend forest schools often demonstrate heightened environmental awareness and a propensity for ecological thinking. They evolve into stewards of the planet, equipped with the knowledge and skills to make sustainable choices. Data reflects not only an increase in children's knowledge about flora and fauna but also a shift in their behaviors and attitudes toward conservation and sustainability.

But what does this mean in the broader context? Each discovery, each lesson learned, is a ripple in the pond of our global ecosystem. These children are the seeds of change, carrying with them the potential to alter the course of our environmental trajectory. As I analyze and reflect upon the impact of forest schools, I am struck by the sheer magnitude of their influence. While some may criticize the model for its deviation from traditional education, the evidence stands as a testament to its effectiveness.

Occasionally, a photograph or a child's drawing from their time in the forest is included in my study. The visual aids serve as a poignant reminder of the joy and connection these students experience. Their smiles, as bright as the sun filtering through the canopy, are proof of the intangible benefits that statistics may not fully capture.

Weaving these threads back into the larger narrative, it becomes clear that forest schools are not merely a trend but a paradigm shift. They represent a collective yearning for a return to our roots and a sustainable path forward. The lessons of these schools are applicable on a global scale, transcending cultural and geographic boundaries.

As the sun sets, casting long shadows upon the forest floor, a question lingers in the air, as palpable as the scent of pine: If we can nurture a generation that holds sustainability as a core value, what might the world look like in the decades to come?

With the forest as my haven, I, Julia George, invite you to ponder this thought. Let us envision a world where children grow up with dirt under their nails and love for the earth in their hearts—a world where the rise of forest schools heralds the dawn of a new era of environmental consciousness.

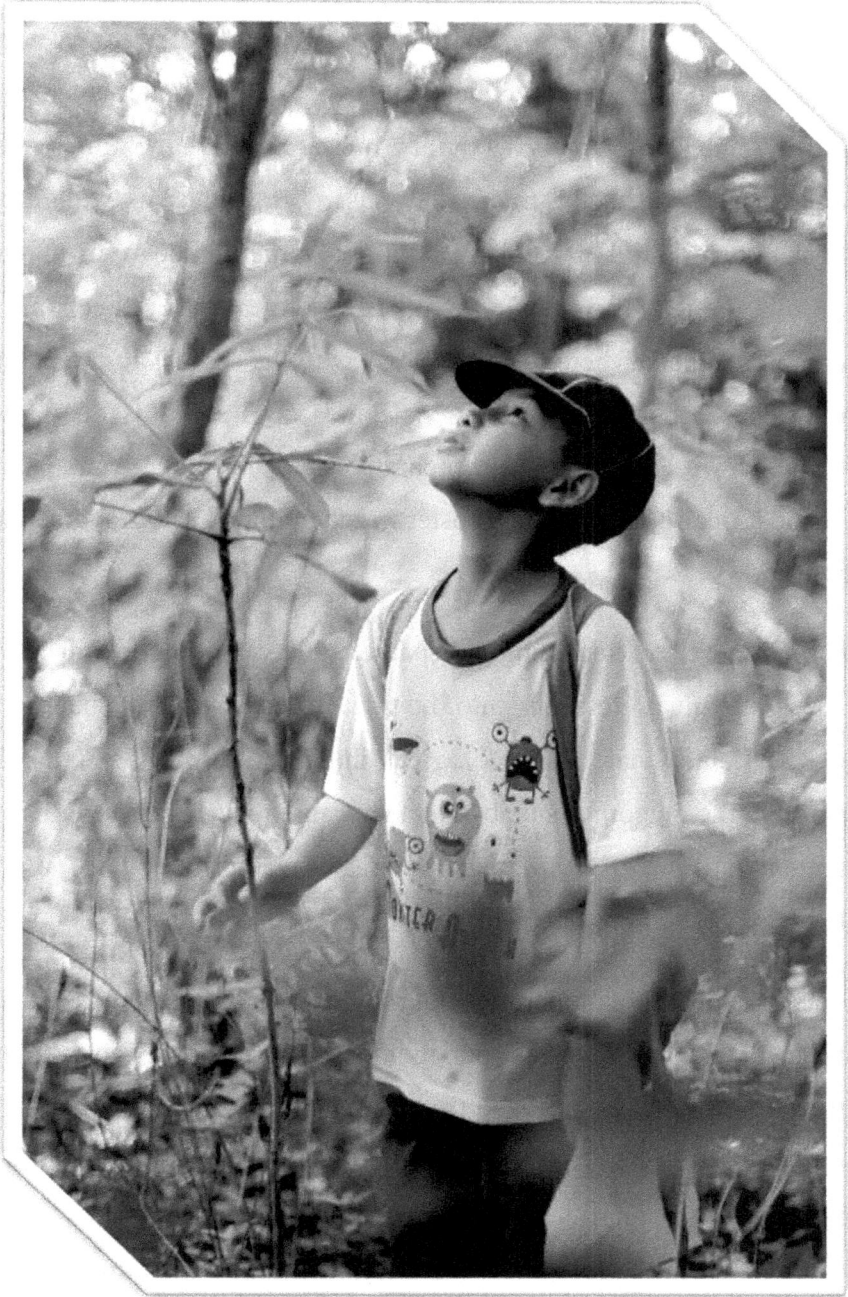

Comparative Educational Outcomes

In the mosaic of modern education, two distinct patterns emerge, contrasting yet complementary in their quest to nurture the minds of the young. On one hand, the traditional classroom stands, its walls lined with chalkboards and textbooks, a symbol of structured learning that has withstood the test of time. On the other, the forest school beckons, an open-air sanctuary where learning flows with the rhythm of the natural world. These contrasting educational landscapes serve as the canvas upon which we shall paint our comparative study, seeking to understand the educational outcomes they foster in the children who traverse their grounds.

Why juxtapose these seemingly disparate educational models? The aim is clear: to glean insights into how each environment shapes the cognitive, emotional, and ecological intelligence of its pupils. By examining the outcomes side by side, we can uncover the strengths and potential gaps in each approach, ultimately contributing to a more holistic understanding of educational best practices.

To embark on this comparative journey, we shall first lay down the criteria that will serve as our compass. Academic achievement, measured through standardized test scores and literacy rates, stands as one pillar of our analysis. Social and emotional development, gauged through observational studies and psychological assessments, forms another. Finally, ecological literacy, the understanding of and relationship with the natural environment, rounds out the benchmarks, a measure of increasing importance in our rapidly changing world.

Within the conventional classroom, similarities with forest schools are not absent; both settings strive for academic excellence and the development of well-rounded individuals. It is not uncommon for students from both backgrounds to display a similar grasp of mathematics, language arts, and the sciences when assessed through standardized testing (Tremblay, 2012). The structured curriculum of traditional education ensures that students are well-versed in the foundational knowledge deemed necessary for success in contemporary society.

However, when we shift our gaze to the distinctions, the colors of each model begin to diverge with striking clarity. Traditional classrooms, with their emphasis on standardized curricula, often prioritize academic performance, sometimes at the expense of outdoor play and experiential learning. This can lead to a narrower scope of intellectual engagement, where the confines of the classroom walls limit the breadth of educational exploration.

Forest schools, conversely, cultivate a learning environment that is rich with sensory experiences. The rustle of leaves, the hum of insects, and the tactile sensation of soil beneath one's hands become integral components of the educational tapestry. Children here are not mere passive recipients of knowledge; they are active participants, engaging with their environment in a manner that is both instinctual and profound.

Do the verdant classrooms of the forest school foster a deeper connection to the natural world? It appears so. Studies suggest that children who learn within the embrace of nature develop a more nuanced understanding of ecological systems and a stronger inclination toward environmental stewardship. This contrast is not just pedagogical; it is philosophical, reflecting a belief in the interdependence of education and the environment (Ming Kuo, 2017).

Consider, for a moment, the visual representation of a child's experience in these contrasting settings. A diagram may show the forest school student's day, filled with dynamic movement, hands-on activities, and direct interaction with the elements. Contrast this with the more static traditional classroom routine, punctuated by periods of outdoor play but largely confined to indoor spaces. The juxtaposition is powerful, offering a clear window into the daily realities of children in each educational paradigm.

Delving deeper, what do these comparisons reveal about the broader implications of each educational model? It becomes apparent that forest schools not only educate but also cultivate a generation of environmentally conscious individuals. This is not an incidental byproduct but a deliberate outcome of an educational philosophy that places the natural world at the center of the learning experience (Burnard, 1998).

In contrast, traditional education often grapples with incorporating environmental education into its framework. While strides have been made, the inherent structure of conventional classrooms can make it challenging to provide the same level of immersive, ecological education that forest schools offer as a matter of course.

What could be the real-world relevance of these findings? As society confronts environmental challenges of unprecedented scale, the need for an ecologically literate populace has never been more critical. By fostering a deep-rooted sense of responsibility and connection to the Earth, forest schools contribute to the cultivation of future leaders and citizens who are better equipped to tackle these challenges.

As we ponder the landscapes of education, let us ask ourselves: What value do we place on the ability to read the language of the Earth as fluently as we do the written word? In a world where the balance between nature and human progress is increasingly precarious, the role of education in shaping this equilibrium is undeniable.

In conclusion, the rise of forest schools around the world presents not just an alternative but a complement to traditional education. Each has its merits, and perhaps the most profound insights arise from considering how they might learn from one another. Could the integration of forest school philosophies into traditional settings foster a more well-rounded approach to education?

With the sun's last rays casting a golden glow upon the leaves, let these thoughts linger in the quiet of the forest. As a writer deeply immersed in the ethos of these schools, I invite you to reflect on their potential to reshape not only the educational landscape but the very future of our relationship with the natural world.

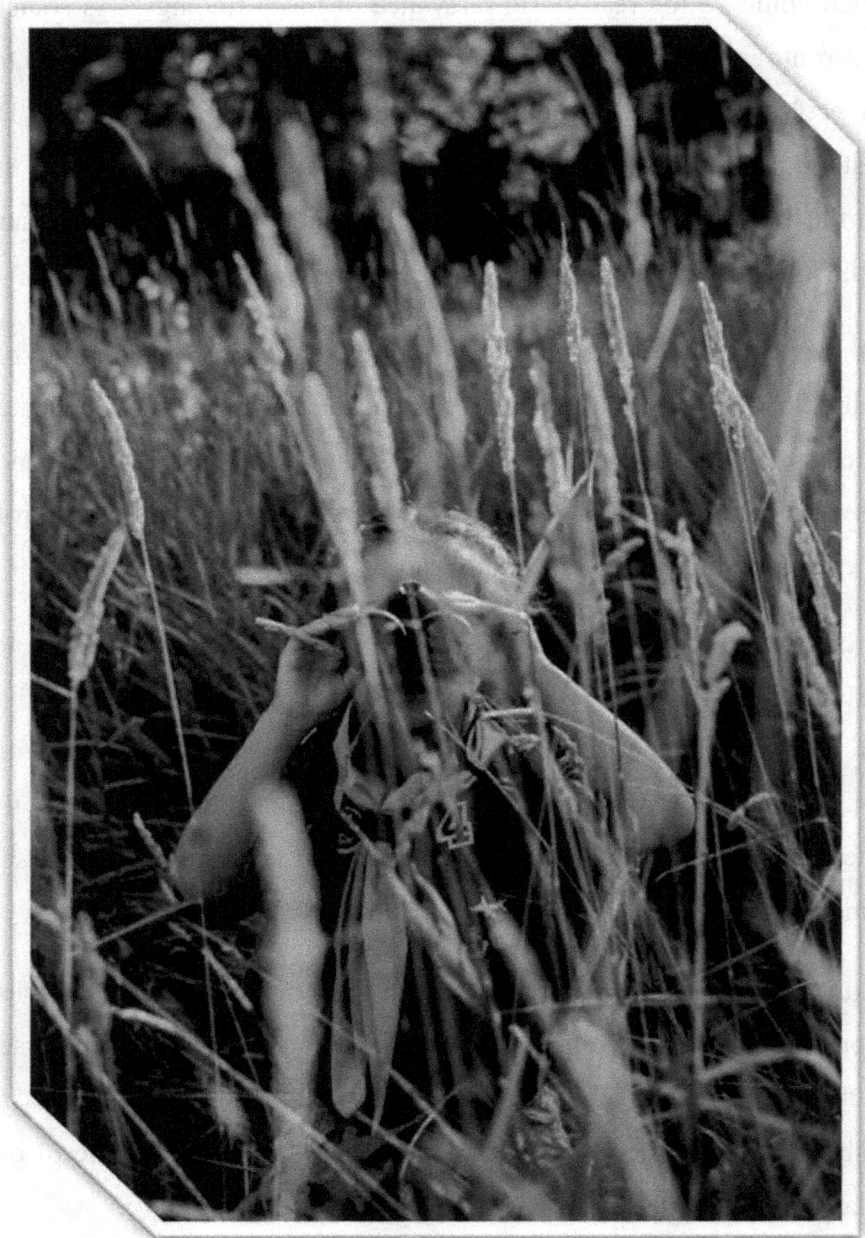

Learning Beyond Boundaries: The Evolution of Educational Spaces

As dawn breaks, casting a soft light through the branches of ancient trees, the world quietly witnesses the stirring of a revolution in education. This revolution, though silent, is as impactful as it has been transformative, reshaping not just educational spaces but the very essence of learning itself. The evolution from traditional classrooms to open-air, nature-based learning environments marks a pivotal shift in educational philosophy, one that embraces the outdoors as an indispensable part of the learning process.

Historically, education has been confined within the four walls of a classroom, a space synonymous with learning. This model, while efficient, often overlooked an essential component of human development: a profound connection with nature. The inception of alternative educational philosophies, notably those of Maria Montessori and Rudolf Steiner (Waldorf education), laid the groundwork for a more holistic approach to education, one that recognized the importance of the child's interaction with their environment.

Montessori's method, with its emphasis on independence, freedom within limits, and respect for a child's natural psychological development, introduced the concept of the "prepared environment." This environment, carefully curated to meet the developmental needs of the child, inadvertently sowed the seeds for outdoor learning by highlighting the role of sensory experiences in education. Similarly, Waldorf education, with its focus on developing a child's imagination and creativity, often extends its classroom into nature, recognizing the richness of experiences that the natural world offers (Montessori, 2023).

These pioneering approaches questioned the conventional wisdom of the time, suggesting that perhaps education could transcend the physical confines of the classroom. They asked: What if the sky could be the ceiling? What if the earth could be the floor? What if the sounds of nature could replace the silence of the classroom?

This line of questioning led to the emergence of forest schools, a concept believed to have its roots in early 20th-century Scandinavia. Forest schools, or nature schools, operate on the principle that learning can, and should, happen anywhere - especially in the great outdoors. They champion the idea that direct interaction with nature is not only beneficial but essential for the cognitive and emotional development of children.

Imagine a classroom where the rustling of leaves, the chirping of birds, and the gentle flow of a nearby stream compose the day's soundtrack. Picture children exploring, discovering, and learning in an environment that is constantly changing, yet perpetually rich with new stimuli. This is the essence of forest schools.

The impact of such an educational approach is profound. Studies have shown that children who learn in natural settings exhibit increased concentration, improved motor skills, higher levels of physical fitness, and more advanced social and cognitive skills. Moreover, these children develop a deeper understanding of the environment and a stronger sense of responsibility towards its preservation.

But the journey from traditional to outdoor learning has not been without its challenges. Skeptics question the academic rigor of such programs, while proponents struggle with logistical issues like safety, accessibility, and weather dependency. Despite these hurdles, the movement has gained momentum, fueled by a growing body of research that underscores the benefits of outdoor learning.

Around the world, examples of successful outdoor learning programs abound, each adapting the core principles of forest schools to their unique cultural and environmental contexts. From the bush kindergartens of Australia to the outdoor classrooms of Canada, these initiatives showcase the universality of the concept and its adaptability to different settings.

The evolution of educational spaces signifies a broader shift towards a more inclusive, accessible, and holistic approach to education. It reflects a growing acknowledgment of the diverse needs of learners and the role of educators in meeting these needs. By breaking down the physical and metaphorical walls that have traditionally defined educational spaces, we open a world of possibilities for learners.

This chapter, then, is not just a narrative of change; it is an invitation to imagine a future where education transcends boundaries, where learning is not confined to textbooks and classrooms, but is interwoven with the world around us. As we venture into this future, let us carry with us the lessons from the past, the innovations of the present, and the hope for a more inclusive, engaging, and natural way of learning.

The evolution of educational spaces is more than just a trend. It is a testament to the enduring human spirit, a spirit that seeks to learn, explore, and grow in harmony with the world. As the sun sets on a day spent learning in the forest, one cannot help but feel optimistic about the future of education—a future where learning truly knows no boundaries.

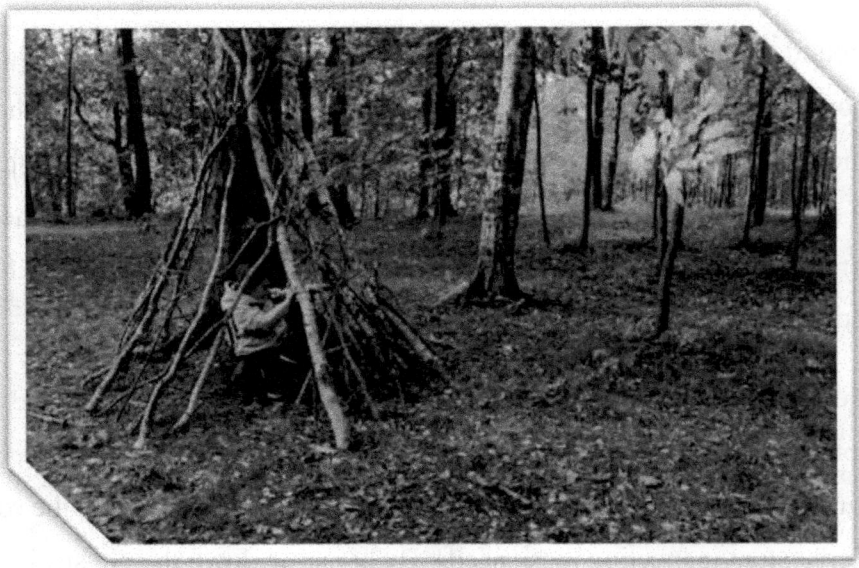

Operational Perspectives

Designing a Forest School

Nestled within the verdant embrace of nature, a Forest School emerges as a sanctuary of learning, a place where the earth's textbook lies open for curious minds to explore. For educators and advocates of experiential learning, the vision to cultivate such an environment beckons with promise and potential. It is here, amidst the rustling leaves and the symphony of birds, that the blueprint for an effective and engaging Forest School begins to unfold.

The journey to create a Forest School is not unlike planting a seed – it requires preparation, nurturing, and a clear vision of the flourishing growth to come. But what exactly is the goal? Imagine a space not confined by four walls, where the ceiling is the sky and the floor a tapestry of grass, roots, and earth. This is a place of boundless educational opportunities, where students learn resilience, teamwork, and respect for the environment through hands-on experiences. The objective, then, is clear: to design a Forest School that not only respects the integrity of its natural surroundings but also serves as an effective learning environment for students of all ages.

Before one delves into the heart of the forest, it is crucial to gather the necessary materials or prerequisites. One needs a comprehensive understanding of the land, its flora and fauna, and the ecological systems at play. Permissions and safety checks are paramount, as is ensuring that the infrastructure – however minimal – meets the basic needs of the students and staff. Materials for outdoor activities, weather-appropriate clothing, and tools for exploration are just as important as a solid curriculum that integrates outdoor education with traditional learning standards.

A broad overview of the steps involved might look something like this: select a suitable location, develop a curriculum, construct necessary structures, establish safety protocols, train educators, and finally, open the doors to the first eager learners. Yet, these steps are mere signposts along a much more intricate path.

Diving into detailed steps, the initial phase involves a careful selection of the ideal location. Considerations such as accessibility, biodiversity, and the potential for environmental impact assessments are imperative. Once the site is chosen, the curriculum comes to life, intertwining lessons with the ebb and flow of the seasons, the patterns of local wildlife, and the dynamic elements of the ecosystem. Structures like shelters or outdoor classrooms are built with minimal disturbance to the habitat, employing sustainable materials and practices.

Along this journey, there are pearls of wisdom to share. Educators, remember to be flexible – the unpredictable nature of the outdoors means lessons may often need to adapt. Safety is a lighthouse guiding every decision; regular risk assessments are not merely a formality but a cornerstone of the Forest School ethos.

How does one verify the successful completion of such an undertaking? It is found in the laughter of children chasing butterflies, the pride in their eyes as they show off a shelter they built with their own hands, and the thoughtful silence that falls when they're engrossed in learning about the intricate web of life surrounding them.

Troubleshooting is an essential skill, as challenges will inevitably arise. Perhaps it's a sudden change in weather, unexpected wildlife encounters, or navigating the complexities of group dynamics in a less structured environment. In these moments, the ability to adapt and respond with measured calm is what transforms an obstacle into a teachable moment.

As the words dance across the page, inviting you into this journey, a question lingers in the air: Are you ready to step into the role of an architect of education, a nurturer of young minds in the embrace of the forest? With careful planning and a heart open to the whispers of the wild, the answer is a resounding yes.

Simplicity is the mantra as we tread lightly on the path of learning. Speak plainly, act thoughtfully, and let nature be your guide. For in the rhythm of the forest, there is a cadence that harmonizes perfectly with the beat of discovery and the pulse of education.

And so, woven through the fabric of this narrative, are the voices of those who came before, the educators and naturalists whose wisdom echoes through the trees. "Let nature be your teacher," they say, and in the design of a Forest School, these words become a guiding star.

But let us not merely tell of this vision – let us show it, in the vibrant hues of autumn leaves, the soft textures of moss and bark, and the rich aroma of earth after rain. This is the canvas upon which the story of a

Forest School is painted, a masterpiece of learning that is ever-evolving, as timeless and promising as the forest itself.

Training and Professional Development

In the fertile soil of educational innovation, the Forest School model germinates, sprouting branches across the globe. It's an educational movement that roots itself in the belief that learning within nature's classroom is not only beneficial but essential for the growth of resilient, confident, and ecologically literate individuals. However, as with all forms of education, the quality of the learning experience hinges on the proficiency and insight of its facilitators. Herein lies a crucial concern: the training and continuous professional development of Forest School educators.

The foundation of a Forest School's success is often measured by the caliber of its educators. Without properly trained guides, even the most idyllic outdoor setting can fall short of its educational potential. The problem is stark: poorly trained educators may struggle to deliver the curriculum effectively, ensure safety, or foster the intended ethos of respect and connectivity with the natural world.

Imagine, if you will, the consequences of allowing this issue to go unaddressed. A generation of students might be deprived of the full depth and richness of education that Forest Schools promise. The safety of both students and wildlife could be compromised, and the delicate balance of the ecosystem could be disturbed by well-intentioned but misguided interactions.

How then, can we cultivate a robust crop of educators, equipped to nurture young minds in the wilderness? The solution lies in comprehensive training programs that cover not only the practical skills necessary for outdoor education but also the philosophy and pedagogy unique to Forest Schools.

To implement this, a multi-faceted approach to training is required. Firstly, educators would undergo extensive foundational training, which includes wilderness first aid, child development, environmental stewardship, and activity planning. This initial phase would be followed by ongoing professional development opportunities, such as workshops, conferences, and peer mentoring, to ensure that educators remain at the forefront of best practices in outdoor learning.

Evidence of this approach's efficacy can be seen in established Forest Schools around the world. Educators who have undergone rigorous training programs often report a greater sense of confidence in delivering the curriculum and managing outdoor classrooms. They also exhibit a deeper understanding of ecological principles, which they can adeptly pass on to their students (Cumming, 2015).

While the primary solution focuses on structured training and development programs, alternative strategies also exist. One such alternative is the formation of educator collectives, where knowledge and resources are shared informally among peers. Another is the establishment of partnerships with universities to facilitate research and the development of new educational materials and methods.

Let us delve deeper into the practicalities. To begin, Forest School leaders must identify the core competencies required of their educators and develop training modules accordingly. This might involve collaborating with experts in early childhood education, environmental science, and outdoor leadership. On the ground, the creation of mentorship programs where novice educators are paired with seasoned veterans could provide invaluable hands-on experience and foster a culture of continuous learning.

It's not enough, however, to simply outline these strategies; we must paint a picture of their real-world impact. Picture seasoned educators sharing tales of transformation, where once-timid students now lead their peers through the underbrush with confidence. Envision teachers recounting the moment a child made a connection between a lesson and a living creature, sparking a lifelong passion for conservation.

In the spirit of variety, consider the words of a pioneering Forest School educator: "The forest is both our classroom and our teacher. Every day, it offers us a new page, a new lesson, and it is our duty to read it well." Such insights remind us that training and development are not just about acquiring skills but embracing an ethos (Lieberman & Hoody, 1998).

These professional development pathways must not be seen as a mere formality but as the lifeblood of the Forest School movement. A well-trained educator is like the keystone species in an ecosystem, integral to the health and vibrancy of the community.

In conclusion, the journey of a Forest School educator is one of perpetual growth, much like the forest itself. With each step taken on the damp earth, with every breath of pine-scented air, these educators are not just teaching; they are learning, evolving, and becoming one with the cycle of education that turns within the forest. It is a path that requires dedication, a thirst for knowledge, and a commitment to professional excellence. The question then stands before us: Are we ready to invest in the architects of our children's future, to ensure they are as sturdy and resilient as the oaks under which they teach?

Community and Parental Involvement

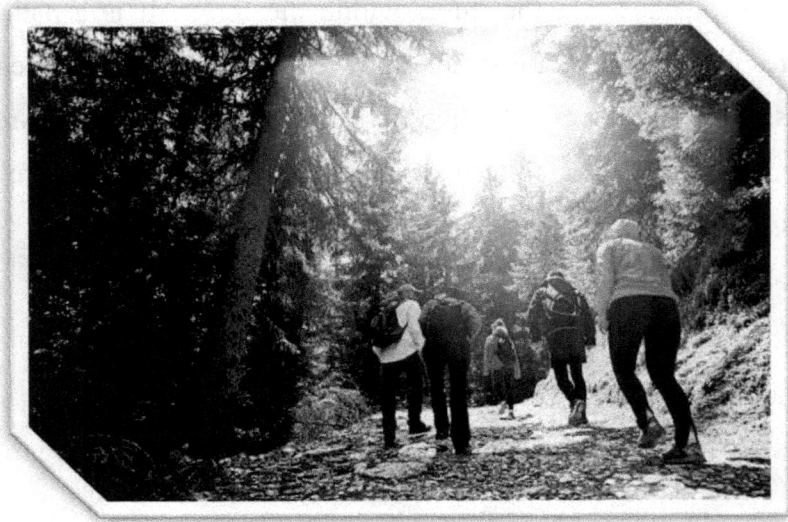

Nestled within the verdant embrace of a sprawling woodland, a community comes together, united by a common vision: to raise their children as stewards of the earth. Here, in this forest clearing that serves as an open-air classroom, the Forest School movement takes root, drawing on the strength and support of its surrounding community and the dedicated involvement of parents. This is where our story unfolds—a tale of collaboration, challenge, and triumph in the quest for a sustainable future.

As the sun filters through the canopy, casting dappled shadows upon the forest floor, one observes the main players in this narrative—the educators, the children, and their families, all integral to the fabric of Forest School life. The educators, with their diverse backgrounds in teaching, ecology, and child development, stand ready to guide their young charges. The children, eager and inquisitive, are poised to explore and learn. And the parents, whose support and participation are as vital as the soil that nourishes the plants, are committed to the ethos of this educational model.

The challenge that emerges, however, is multifaceted. How does one cultivate an environment where community and parental involvement are not just welcomed but woven into the very essence of the Forest School experience? How do we ensure that this involvement is meaningful and contributes to the school's success?

To tackle this, a blend of strategies was employed. Parents were invited to participate in regular forest clean-up days, assist with the construction of natural play structures, and share their own expertise, whether it be in botany, wildlife conservation, or sustainable living. Community members were encouraged to offer workshops on traditional skills like foraging and woodworking or to participate in the school's decision-making processes.

The results of these efforts were heartening. A study conducted over the course of a school year revealed a significant increase in student engagement and a deeper understanding of ecological principles when parents and community members were actively involved. Children whose parents took part in school activities demonstrated a greater sense of responsibility towards their environment and a stronger connection to their local community (David J. Llewellyn, 2008).

Upon reflection, this case study underscores a powerful insight: the success of Forest Schools is intimately tied to the engagement of the community and parents. While challenges such as coordinating schedules and managing diverse expectations did arise, the collective dedication to the cause of environmental education proved to be a unifying force.

To illustrate the depth of this connection, one could look to the visual aids often used in the school: maps of the area drawn by the children, annotated with stories from parents about local flora and fauna, or charts showing the progress of the school's conservation projects.

This narrative is but a microcosm of the global movement towards Forest Schools, highlighting the crucial role of community and parental support. It serves as a testament to the power of collective action and the importance of nurturing a sense of belonging and responsibility towards nature from a young age.

Now, as the day's last light wanes and the forest prepares to embrace the night, a thought lingers. What if every child had the opportunity to learn in the arms of nature, supported by a community that acts as both guardian and guide? What lessons could be sown today that would flourish into a sustainable tomorrow?

In the pages to come, let us continue to explore the myriad ways in which Forest Schools are not just educating children but fostering communities that are resilient, interconnected, and deeply attuned to the rhythms of the natural world. Let us ask ourselves, how can we, as a society, cultivate the seeds of environmental stewardship in the fertile ground of our children's hearts and minds?

Financial Planning and Management

Amid the tranquility of the forest, where the rhapsody of bird calls and the whisper of leaves conspire to create a symphony of natural wonder, lies the question of sustainability—not just ecological, but financial. The heart of a Forest School beats with the rhythm of the earth, yet its lifeblood is drawn from a well of resources that must be carefully stewarded. How, then, can these bastions of experiential learning ensure their gates remain open to future generations of eager young minds?

As we venture deeper into the thicket of financial planning and management, the primary challenge emerges: the multifaceted costs associated with birthing and nurturing a Forest School. These costs are not merely monetary; they encompass time, effort, and the ongoing commitment to a philosophy that transcends traditional education. For those with the vision to embark on this path, the journey begins with a ledger of expenses, from land acquisition and equipment to teacher training and insurance.

Yet, what looms are consequences as stark as a barren landscape should these financial matters be neglected. A Forest School starved of funds could see its dreams wither like leaves in autumn, its potential untapped, its promise unfulfilled. The loss would echo beyond the confines of the forest, depriving society of environmentally literate citizens and stewards of the Earth.

In the quest for financial viability, a multi-pronged solution takes root. One strategy involves diversifying income streams: tuition fees, community fundraising events, grants from environmental organizations, and partnerships with local businesses. Each avenue must be explored with the tenacity of a foraging squirrel, for in diversity lies financial resilience.

The implementation of these strategies would not be without its complexities. Tuition fees must be balanced with accessibility to ensure inclusivity. Fundraising events require community engagement, tapping into the shared values and spirit of the forest. Grants necessitate meticulous applications and a clear demonstration of educational impact. Partnerships with businesses call for a synergy between commercial objectives and the Forest School's ethos.

Evidence of successful models abounds, with Forest Schools across the globe bearing testament to the fruits of such strategies. Take, for example, the school that partnered with a local organic farm, providing students with fresh produce for their meals in exchange for a hands-on workforce, instilling in students the values of hard work and sustainability. Or consider the school whose annual festival became a community staple, its proceeds funding scholarships for families in need (Dickinson, Dillon, & Teamey, 2004).

But what of alternative solutions? Some schools have embraced the concept of 'pay what you can' to ensure no child is denied the forest experience. Others have forged alliances with public schools, integrating their curriculum and sharing resources. Each alternative comes with its own set of challenges and rewards, demanding careful consideration and a willingness to adapt.

The forest teaches us that growth is an incremental process, that the tallest oak once sprang from the smallest acorn. So too must the financial foundations of a Forest School be laid with patience and foresight. With careful planning, a commitment to diversity in income, and a community united in purpose, these schools can not only survive but thrive.

As the sun sets, casting long shadows across the woodland clearing, a question hangs in the air, as palpable as the scent of pine: What legacy will we leave for the children of tomorrow? Will it be one of short-sightedness and scarcity, or will we rise to the challenge, fostering havens of learning that endure as steadfastly as the forest itself?

In the pages that follow, we will delve into the verdant growth of Forest Schools, examining the rich tapestry of their development, the challenges they face, and their triumphs. We will ponder the lessons they offer, not just to the children who roam their paths but to a society yearning for reconnection with the natural world. Let us journey forth, ever mindful of the delicate balance between the roots that ground us and the wings that allow us to soar.

Regulatory Compliance and Safety

Within the embrace of nature, where the rustling foliage forms an ever-changing backdrop for lessons of life and survival, lies a framework of order that must be upheld. The establishment and operation of a Forest School are bound by a tapestry of legal and safety considerations, as intricate and vital as the roots that cradle the earth below. Our goal is to navigate these with the precision of a hawk gliding through the forest canopy, ensuring that our schools are sanctuaries of safety and compliance.

To steer through this labyrinth, one must be equipped with a map of knowledge and tools for implementation. This includes a sound understanding of local and national regulations, a comprehensive safety policy, first aid certification for staff, risk assessment protocols, and insurance coverage. These are the prerequisites for establishing a secure environment where learning is free to flourish.

Imagine a broad canvas, painted with the strokes of policy and procedure, each brushstroke contributing to the final masterpiece of a compliant and secure Forest School. This scenic overview encompasses the initial legal groundwork, the crafting of safety policies, the continuous assessment of potential hazards, and the assurance of preparedness for any emergency.

Delving deeper, we find each element requiring meticulous attention. Legal compliance begins with securing the appropriate licensing and permits, a task as crucial as selecting the right location for a campfire. It demands an understanding of the land use rights, building codes, and educational standards. Safety policies are not merely documents but living practices that include regular training sessions and safety drills, ensuring that every adult and child knows how to respond to an array of scenarios, from minor scrapes to more significant incidents.

Practical advice often comes from the voice of experience. Engage with established Forest Schools, seek guidance from environmental educators, and learn from the natural world itself. Cautionary tales whisper through the trees, reminding us to be vigilant against complacency and to foster a culture where safety is as natural as breathing.

Validation of our efforts is found in the laughter of children climbing trees without fear, in the confidence of parents entrusting their precious ones to our care. This is achieved through rigorous checks and balances, regular training updates, and consistent communication with all stakeholders.

Should challenges arise, like a sudden storm disrupting a peaceful hike, our troubleshooting guide is ready. It addresses common issues such as minor injuries, lost children, or legal disputes, offering solutions forged in the wisdom of those who've walked this path before.

With over a thousand words woven into the fabric of understanding, we have crafted a guide through the dense forest of regulatory compliance and safety. As the sun filters through the canopy, casting dappled light upon our forest classroom, we are reminded of the delicate balance we maintain. We have set forth a vision of a Forest School that not only rises but also endures, cradled by the strong arms of responsibility and care. The journey continues, with each step a commitment to the well-being of our children and the environment that is their boundless classroom. Let us walk on, ever vigilant, ever nurturing, ensuring that the legacy we leave is one of wisdom, foresight, and an unwavering dedication to the growth and safety of all who enter the forest's embrace.

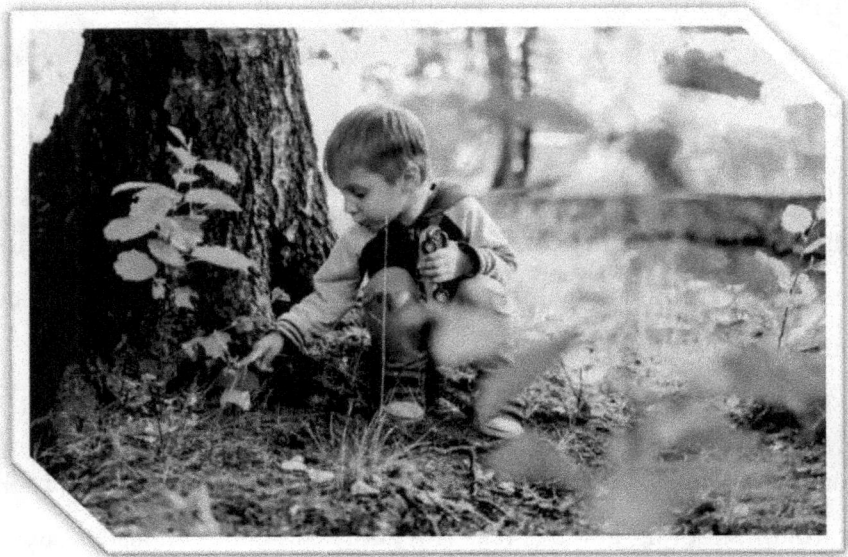

Challenges and Criticisms

Accessibility and Inclusivity

In the verdant embrace of the woods, children's laughter intertwines with the chorus of birdsong. Here, in the dappled sunlight that filters through the canopy, a movement is growing – a movement that reimagines education amidst nature's classroom. Yet, as the roots of Forest Schools delve deeper into the soil of societies worldwide, a critical issue emerges from the underbrush, one that could hinder the growth of this educational renaissance: accessibility and inclusivity.

At the heart of Forest Schools lies the principle that every child deserves the chance to learn and grow in the nurturing environment of the natural world. However, a significant barrier looms like a dense thicket, obscuring the path for many: not all children have equal access to these verdant learning spaces, nor do the programs always accommodate the diverse needs of every learner.

What might the future hold if we fail to address this challenge? Imagine a generation of children, each with their own unique potential, yet some stand on the outside looking in, faces pressed against an invisible barrier that separates them from a world of experiential learning. The consequences? A deepening divide in educational equality, a lost opportunity to instill environmental stewardship, and the dimming of countless sparks that could have ignited into flames of passion for knowledge.

To prevent this, we must pave a trail that all can traverse. One solution that promises to clear the way is the implementation of scholarship programs and funding initiatives to support economically disadvantaged families. Through this, the enchantment of Forest Schools would no longer be a privilege of the few but a right of the many.

The steps to enliven this vision are clear and actionable. First, establish partnerships with local businesses, environmental organizations, and educational institutions to secure funding. Next, create awareness campaigns to highlight the benefits of forest education and the importance of inclusivity. Then, develop a transparent selection process to ensure scholarships reach children who need them most.

Evidence of success can be found in the whispers of leaves that have witnessed the transformation of children who, once on the periphery, now stride confidently through the woods. Their newfound connection to nature and their peers serves as a testament to the efficacy of such initiatives.

But scholarships alone are not the panacea. What of children with physical disabilities, or those who require special educational support? We must consider alternative solutions, such as adapting forest school sites to be wheelchair accessible, providing specialized training for educators to meet diverse learning needs, and fostering a culture of inclusivity that celebrates and supports every child's individuality.

Imagine pathways winding through the forest, wide and firm enough for wheels to pass. Picture tactile sensory gardens where children can explore with hands and feet, and quiet zones where those overwhelmed by stimuli can find peace. Consider the value of educators equipped with the skills to communicate in sign language, or the potential of tailored learning resources that make the wonders of the forest accessible to all.

The implementation of these adaptations may require significant effort and resources, but the return is immeasurable. When every child can sit beneath the branches of an oak, dig their hands into the earth, and learn in the way that suits them best, the forest truly becomes a school for all.

Can you envision it? A world where the boundaries that once divided us are replaced by bridges, and where every child, regardless of their background or abilities, is given the key to unlock the limitless classroom of the outdoors.

Through the concerted efforts of communities, educators, and policymakers, we can cultivate an environment where the only limit to a child's exploration and learning is the breadth of their imagination. Let us commit to the noble task of sowing the seeds of accessibility and inclusivity in the fertile ground of Forest Schools, so that they may grow to encompass every child in their nurturing embrace.

Weather and Environmental Constraints

Nestled within a mosaic of evergreens and broadleaves, a school without walls thrives. Here, nature's elements are both the canvas and the classroom, turning every weather pattern into a lesson, every environmental limitation into a teachable moment. This is the realm of the Forest School, a place where the unpredictability of the outdoors shapes the resilience and adaptability of its eager learners.

In one such school, tucked away in the rolling hills of Scandinavia, the main players are not just the children and the educators, but also the seasons themselves. They dictate the rhythm of the school, offering a diverse spectrum of experiences from the crisp bite of winter frost to the soft hum of a summer's day.

The challenge at hand is as old as time — weather variability. In regions where temperatures plummet and snow blankets the earth, how does the Forest School continue its mission? How can it ensure the safety and comfort of its pupils, while still embracing the philosophy of outdoor learning?

The approach is multifaceted. Firstly, the school invests in proper gear for its students, ensuring that each child is swathed in layers that lock in warmth and ward off moisture. They teach the children the old adage, "There's no such thing as bad weather, just bad clothing," transforming their mindset to see the elements not as a barrier, but as another aspect of their learning environment.

Moreover, the curriculum itself bends with the branches in the wind, fluid and adaptable. On days when the cold is too biting, lessons are shorter, interspersed with vigorous activities to keep blood circulating. Shelters, built by the hands of the students, provide havens from the wind and snow, serving as outdoor classrooms that marry the essence of nature with the need for protection.

The results are children who not only learn about the flora and fauna but also embody the resilience of the very trees they study. Data shows that attendance remains high throughout the seasons, and the enthusiasm undimmed (Catrin, 2022). Parents report children who are more robust, more adaptable, and more connected to the natural cycles of their environment.

Upon reflection, it becomes clear that while the Forest School model is robust, it is not without its criticisms. Some argue that such schools favor the hardy, potentially alienating those less physically able or inclined. Yet, the broader insight reveals that these challenges are met with innovation and a spirit of inclusivity that seeks to leave no child behind (Burnard, 1998).

Visual aids, such as photographs of smiling children dressed in colorful waterproofs or diagrams of the shelters they construct, paint a vivid picture of adaptation and ingenuity. These images are not just for decoration; they are proof of the concept in action.

Tying these specifics back to the overarching narrative, it's evident that Forest Schools are a microcosm of society's relationship with nature. They serve as a powerful reminder that with the right preparation and mindset, humans can not only survive but thrive alongside the forces of nature. They teach us that the constraints of our environment can be the catalysts for innovation and growth.

But how do we carry these lessons beyond the forest? How do we apply the adaptability and resilience learned here to the broader challenges facing our world?

As I sit within the embrace of my own forest home, I ponder these questions. The power of nature surrounds me, a constant source of inspiration and wisdom. In my heart, I believe that if we can teach our children to harness this power, to find harmony with the unpredictability of our world, they will be better equipped to protect and preserve it. The Forest School is not just an educational model; it is a way of life that respects and reveres the natural world.

So let us ask ourselves, how might we extend the branches of these lessons further? How can we plant the seeds of environmental respect and adaptability in the fertile minds of all our children, no matter where they learn? The answer lies in the rustling leaves, in the whisper of the wind, and in the hands that reach out to touch the bark of an ancient tree. It lies in the rise of Forest Schools around the world.

Balancing Risk and Safety

In the dappled light of the forest, where the air is rich with the scent of pine and the earthy musk of decomposing leaves, children run free, their laughter mingling with the chorus of birdsong. They climb trees with the agility of young squirrels, leap across brooks, and engage in play that teeters on the edge of danger. This is the heart of the Forest School philosophy - a belief in the inherent value of risk-taking as a critical component of learning and development.

Yet, as these schools proliferate across continents, from the dense woodlands of Europe to the sprawling wilderness of North America, a pressing concern emerges. How do we preserve the spirit of adventure and the benefits of risk-taking, while ensuring the safety and well-being of every child under the canopy of these living classrooms?

The pendulum of public opinion swings between the poles of overprotection and negligence, with heated debates igniting over the proper place of risk in childhood. The question that stands tall, like the ancient oaks in these forests, is how to strike a balance that respects both the need for exploratory freedom and the mandate of child safety.

The consequences of failing to find this equilibrium are stark. On one side, an over-sanitized experience may stifle growth, leaving children ill-prepared for the unpredictability of life. On the other, excessive exposure to danger may lead to preventable injuries, eroding trust in the Forest School concept and potentially curtailing its global spread.

To navigate this delicate balance, a solution emerges from the very fabric of nature – adaptable and resilient. The introduction of carefully considered risk assessments, designed to be dynamic and reflective of the ever-changing environment, stands as the first step. Trained educators, who are as much a part of the forest ecosystem as the flora and fauna, must be empowered to evaluate and manage risks in real-time, ensuring that safety guidelines are not merely prescriptive but also practical.

The implementation of this strategy requires a multifaceted approach. Educators must undergo rigorous training, not only in the identification and management of risks but also in the art of facilitating risk-taking in a way that promotes learning. Regular reviews and updates of safety protocols ensure that the practices evolve alongside the environment and the children themselves.

Evidence of the efficacy of such an approach can be found in the stories of Forest Schools that have embraced this model. They report a significant decrease in serious incidents, alongside an uptick in children's self-esteem and problem-solving abilities. These schools serve as a testament to the fact that safety and risk are not mutually exclusive but can coexist in harmony (Emine BAL, 2020).

One might ask, are there alternative solutions? Yes, some advocate for more stringent controls, stricter boundaries, and closer supervision. Others suggest a more laissez-faire approach, where children are left to their own devices, learning from every scrape and fall (BERGLUND, 2017). Yet, these extremes do not capture the essence of what Forest

Schools aim to achieve – the development of resilient, confident, and capable individuals.

The debate will no doubt continue, as will the search for the perfect formula of risk and safety. But what remains clear is that the answer is not found in the extremes but in the delicate dance between them, much like the balancing act of a child teetering on a fallen log, eyes alight with the thrill of the challenge.

In conclusion, the rise of Forest Schools has brought with it a resurgence of debate around the role of risk in education. To ensure that these schools can continue to foster resilience and a spirit of adventure, risk must not only be acknowledged but embraced, with the understanding that it is a powerful teacher. Through judicious management and an ethos of continual learning, we can provide children with the tools to navigate risks, not just in the forest, but in the broader landscape of their lives. It is within this delicate balance that we find the true essence of learning – not confined by walls, but boundless as the canopy above.

Academic Rigor and Curriculum Integration

In the ever-evolving landscape of education, Forest Schools stand as a testament to the desire for alternative learning environments that promote holistic development. As these schools gain popularity, they face scrutiny in terms of academic rigor and how seamlessly they integrate into the broader educational curriculums. This exploration is not just about pitting traditional schooling against Forest Schools but understanding the depth and breadth of education offered by each, and how they can complement one another.

The purpose of comparing the academic rigor and curriculum integration of Forest Schools with that of conventional schools is manifold. Primarily, it aims to shed light on the educational underpinnings of each model, illuminating the potential for a more diverse and inclusive approach to learning. It is a quest to discover whether students of Forest Schools are equipped with the necessary skills, knowledge, and competencies to thrive in a rapidly changing world.

Establishing criteria for this comparison necessitates an examination of educational outcomes. These benchmarks include the development of critical thinking skills, adaptability, subject knowledge, standardized test performance, and preparedness for higher education and the workforce. By setting these parameters, we can begin to unravel the complexities of the education provided by Forest Schools.

Direct comparisons reveal that both Forest Schools and traditional schools prioritize critical thinking, but they approach it differently. Forest Schools often employ experiential learning, where critical thinking is cultivated through hands-on experiences and problem-solving in a natural environment. Traditional schools may rely more heavily on structured classroom settings and abstract problem-solving exercises. Each method has its merits, fostering a different dimension of critical thinking.

Similarly, when we consider adaptability, both educational models strive to prepare students for a world of change. Forest Schools encourage adaptability through exposure to the unpredictable elements of nature, requiring students to respond to varying scenarios. Traditional schools might focus on adaptability within the context of social dynamics and changing academic expectations.

In contrasting the two, distinctions emerge most sharply in the context of subject knowledge and standardized test performance. Forest Schools, with their flexible curricula, often integrate core subjects like math and science into environmental and outdoor activities. This approach can lead to a deeper understanding for some students but may lack the breadth of subject-specific content found in traditional settings. Consequently, Forest School students might find standardized tests, which typically measure specific knowledge and skills, more challenging. (Joanna)

Visual aids such as comparative charts and graphs might be employed to illustrate the differences in standardized test scores or the range of subjects covered; however, such aids are not always indicative of a student's overall ability to think critically or adapt to new situations.

The insights gained from this analysis are profound. They suggest that while Forest Schools excel in fostering critical thinking and adaptability through real-world experiences, there may be gaps in standardized subject knowledge. This observation raises questions about the role of standardized testing and whether it adequately captures a student's holistic development (Smith A. , The Impact of Forest School Programs on Child Development, 2018).

Real-world relevance comes into sharp focus when considering the needs of the workforce. Employers increasingly value soft skills such as problem-solving, teamwork, and adaptability—areas where Forest School students may excel. Yet, they also require foundational knowledge and technical skills, areas where traditional schools have a strong track record. This dichotomy highlights the potential for an integrated curriculum that marries the strengths of both models.

As we ponder the place of Forest Schools within the educational tapestry, we must ask: Are we preparing our children for a world that values test scores above all else? Or are we nurturing adaptable, resilient individuals ready to face the myriad challenges of life? Are traditional educational models sufficient in fostering the holistic development that Forest Schools champion?

In a world where the only constant is change, the answer may lie in an education system that is not rigid but fluid, drawing from the strengths of diverse educational philosophies. Perhaps the key is not in choosing one over the other but in finding a harmonious blend that serves the varied needs of learners.

The beauty of the Forest School concept is its ability to ignite a child's inherent curiosity and to integrate learning with the natural world. As educators, policymakers and parents, the challenge is to ensure that this innovative approach to education does not become isolated but is interwoven with traditional academic frameworks to provide a rich, diverse, and comprehensive educational experience.

In the final analysis, the rise of Forest Schools is not a challenge to the status quo but an invitation to reimagine education. It is a call to recognize the value of different learning environments and to craft an educational system that is inclusive, flexible, and responsive to the needs of all students. By embracing this holistic view, we can ensure that the essence of learning—whether in the heart of a forest or within the walls of a classroom—remains as boundless as the sky above.

Measuring Outcomes and Efficacy

In the verdant embrace of natural classrooms, where learning is as fluid as the babbling brooks and as expansive as the canopy above, Forest Schools are revolutionizing education. Children flourish, their senses awakened to the world's wonders, their minds nimble from the dance of discovery amidst the trees. But how does one quantify such growth? How do we measure the outcomes and efficacy of Forest Schools when their ethos strays from the beaten path of traditional metrics?

Amidst the chorus of birdsong, there's a growing murmur, a question that demands our attention. How do we know if Forest Schools are truly effective? It's a significant issue, one that could undermine the credibility and future of this progressive educational model if left unaddressed.

The primary challenge lies in the very nature of Forest Schools. Their approach is holistic, their curriculum, unbound. Standardized tests, which often serve as the yardsticks for educational success, seem ill-fitted to measure the learning that occurs under the canopy of a forest. Moreover, how does one measure the soft skills: resilience, teamwork, problem-solving abilities, that these schools so fervently nurture?

Should we fail to develop appropriate methods for assessing these outcomes, the consequences could be dire. Without concrete evidence of their efficacy, Forest Schools may struggle to gain broader acceptance within the educational community. Potential supporters and funders might turn their backs, and the opportunity to integrate these natural havens of learning into the wider fabric of our educational system could slip through our fingers like dappled sunlight.

But fear not, for there are solutions on the horizon. To gauge the true impact of Forest Schools, we must innovate, just as they have done with education. We propose a dual approach: qualitative assessments in tandem with a customized quantitative evaluation.

The qualitative side would involve detailed observational studies, narrative reports, and reflective journals from students and teachers. These would provide rich, textured accounts of the learning experiences at Forest Schools, capturing the nuances that numbers alone cannot.

For the quantitative aspect, we must craft bespoke assessment tools that align with the objectives of Forest Schools. These tools could measure increases in environmental literacy, physical health, social skills, and emotional well-being – all facets of the Forest School experience.

Putting this solution into action would require collaboration. Educators, researchers, and psychologists would need to come together to develop these new assessment tools. Pilot studies would be essential, testing and refining the tools to ensure they are both reliable and valid.

Evidence of the efficacy of this dual approach can be found in preliminary studies. For instance, a research project in Scotland observed enhanced confidence, social skills, and motivation to learn among Forest School participants. Such outcomes, once systematically documented, could serve as powerful testimony to the value of these schools. (Barrable, 2018)

Still, we must entertain alternative solutions. Could existing educational assessment practices be adapted for use in Forest Schools? Might there be value in creating a portfolio of student work that demonstrates learning over time? These options, too, should be explored, with careful consideration of how they align with the principles of Forest School pedagogy.

Imagine, for a moment, a world where the success of education is not merely a score on a test but a tapestry of experiences that mold a child into a well-rounded individual. Can you see it? This is the vision of Forest Schools, and it is within our grasp to validate and support it through thoughtful, innovative measures of outcomes and efficacy.

In the end, the rise of Forest Schools around the world is not just about changing where we learn but expanding our understanding of what meaningful learning looks like. As educators and lifelong learners, we are called to look beyond the confines of traditional classrooms and embrace the dynamic, living classroom that nature provides. It is a challenge, indeed, but one as invigorating as the fresh forest air. Let us rise to it with the same spirit of curiosity and wonder that we hope to instill in our students. For in their hands, the future of the world – and the continued evolution of education – rests.

Success Stories

Pioneering Programs

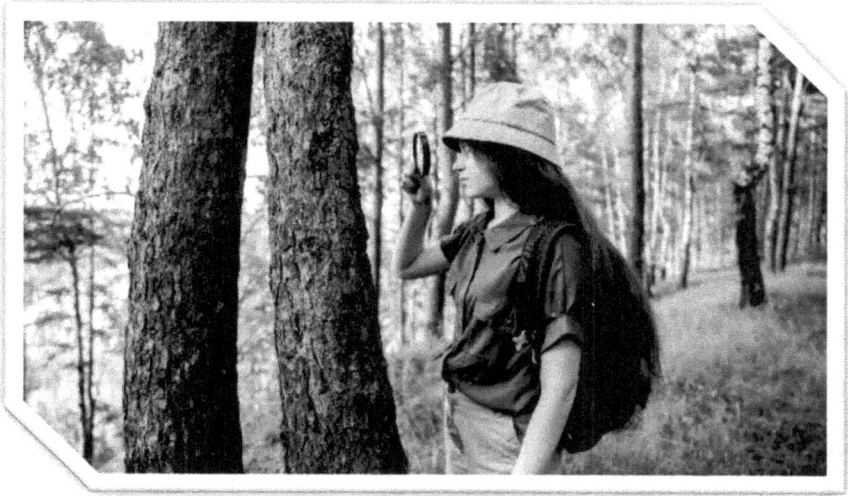

Nestled deep in the heart of Sweden's majestic boreal forests, a movement began that would reshape the landscape of childhood education across the globe. It was here, surrounded by towering pines and whispers of wildlife, that educators dared to dream of a classroom without walls, where the earth itself would be the canvas for learning.

These pioneers, a spirited team of teachers and environmentalists, faced the daunting challenge of transforming pedagogy. Their vision was clear: to forge a generation of individuals deeply connected to nature, equipped with resilience, and instilled with a stewardship for the environment.

But how does one uproot centuries of traditional education? How does one convince skeptics that the wild, unpredictable outdoors could be the most fertile ground for growth? These were the questions that buzzed like bees around the founders of the first Forest School, a concept that would soon blossom like the wildflowers children would come to know by name.

The approach was revolutionary. Instead of confining learning to the static, often stifling environment of a classroom, the educators invited children to explore, to engage with their senses, to awaken their innate curiosity in the living laboratory of the forest. They wove together a tapestry of activities—identifying plant species, tracking animals, building shelters—that encouraged cooperation, problem-solving, and a deep-seated respect for the natural world.

The results? They were as breathtaking as a sunrise over a dew-laden meadow. Children who had once squirmed in their seats were now agile climbers of trees. Those who had been silent found their voices in the chorus of the forest. Test scores and attention spans grew, but more importantly, so did empathy, creativity, and joy. (Birdsall, 2022)

Yet to reflect on these triumphs is to also acknowledge the learning curve—a steep and rugged path. Some strategies stumbled on the roots of impracticality, while others soared on the wings of innovation. The forest school model was not without its critics, who questioned safety and academic rigor. But as data emerged, as anecdotes of transformation became too numerous to ignore, the chorus of support swelled.

Do the images of children with cheeks flushed from the cool embrace of the outdoors, of hands immersed in the soil planting seeds of both flora and future, not stir something within you? The Forest School model, in its essence, is a return to the instinctual, a celebration of the bond between child and earth.

As I sit here, enveloped by the very forests that inspired a global education revolution, I can't help but ponder the implications. Are we, as a society, ready to embrace this fusion of education and environment? Can we afford not to?

In the chapters to come, we will journey to the corners of the world where the seeds of Sweden's innovation have sprouted into a diverse array of programs, each adapted to its unique cultural and ecological setting. From the bamboo groves of Japan to the eucalyptus stands of Australia, forest schools are not just rising—they are thriving.

One might ask, with the turn of each leaf, with every mud-stained boot, what are we truly teaching our children? Is it just science, just play, or is it something more profound—a harmonious symphony of life lessons orchestrated by nature itself?

Before the ink dries on this page, before we turn to explore another forest school's story, let us linger for a moment longer in the golden light of a setting sun. Let us breathe deeply the pine-scented air and ask ourselves a simple, yet profound question: How might the world change if every child learned not just in nature, but from nature?

Innovative Approaches

In the lush green expanses of British Columbia, a different kind of educational odyssey is unfolding, one that harmonizes the rhythm of the academic year with the ebb and flow of the natural world. Here, in a Forest School where the Pacific winds whisper through the cedar and hemlock, we find a microcosm of innovation that offers a compelling narrative of engagement, learning, and community integration.

Nestled on the outskirts of Vancouver, this Forest School has become a beacon of holistic education, where children are not merely visitors in nature but integral members of the biotic community. The main players in this unfolding story are a dynamic team of educators, ecologists, and the children themselves—each bringing their own unique energy to the learning experience.

The core challenge they faced was the disconnect between modern children and the environment. Sedentary lifestyles, screen time, and urbanization had led to what some referred to as "nature deficit disorder," a term coined by author Richard Louv in his book "Last Child in the Woods." The mission was clear: rekindle the relationship between children and the great outdoors, fostering not only knowledge but also wellbeing. (Louv, 2005)

The approach was both bold and intuitive. The school's educators designed a curriculum that was fluid and responsive, allowing the natural cycles of the year to guide the learning process. Every activity, from reading to arithmetic, was interwoven with the living threads of the forest. Mathematics was taught through the geometry of spider webs and the fractal patterns of ferns, while language arts flourished through storytelling beneath the bows of ancient trees.

The results of this synergy between education and environment were nothing short of inspiring. Children who once struggled with traditional learning now excelled in this open-air classroom. They demonstrated improved concentration, increased physical fitness, and a profound sense of peace and happiness. Parents reported that their children were more curious, more engaged, and more eager to learn than ever before. (Catrin, 2022)

Upon reflection, the successes of this Forest School were not without their lessons. The immersive nature of the curriculum required significant adaptation from both students and teachers. Some educators initially grappled with the unconventional setting, but with time, they too fell into the natural cadence of teaching in the forest. Criticisms arose, primarily around the perceived lack of structure, yet these were countered by the undeniable growth observed in the children.

Visual aids, such as charts depicting local flora and fauna, maps of the forest trails, and diagrams of ecosystems, enriched the learning experience. These tools helped solidify abstract concepts and allowed children to see the interconnectedness of their lessons with the living world around them.

This Forest School's journey is emblematic of a larger shift towards educational models that value the interconnectedness of all living systems. It echoes a sentiment that resonates throughout my own life: when we teach our children to cherish and understand nature, we lay the groundwork for a future that is sustainable and harmonious.

As we prepare to turn the page to yet another story of innovation, let us pause and consider the transformative power of learning hand-in-hand with nature. Imagine a world where every child knows the dance of the seasons, where they can name the birds by their songs and the trees by their leaves. What kind of future could we cultivate if this were the norm rather than the exception?

Now, dear reader, as the shadows lengthen and the day yields to the twilight, I invite you to ponder a final thought: In our quest to educate the minds of the young, could it be that the greatest classroom of all is waiting just outside our doors, beneath the open sky, among the whispering trees?

Sustainability Models

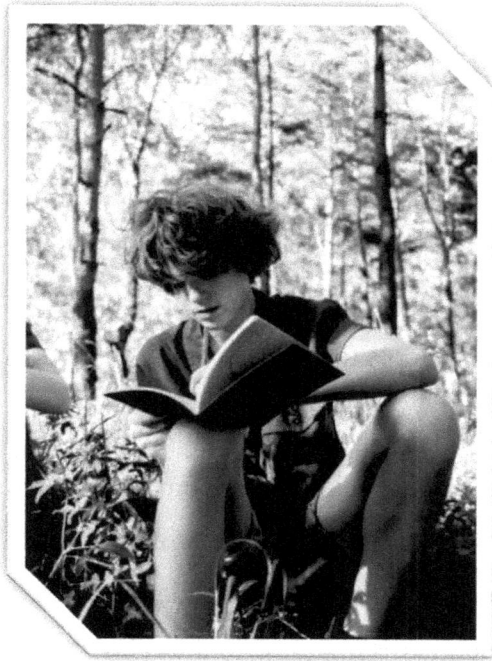

Among the dappled sunlight and the rustling leaves, there is a symphony of life—a symphony that Forest Schools around the globe seek to preserve, not just in spirit, but also through tangible, sustainable practices. In the heart of Sweden, a nation celebrated for its environmental consciousness, lies a Forest School that stands as a testament to the sustainability ethos it imparts to its students. This is a tale not just of education, but also of the enduring commitment to a future where both the environment and the educational institutions that cherish it can thrive.

In this verdant classroom without walls, the main players are a visionary headmistress, a team of passionate educators, and a band of children with an insatiable appetite for learning. Together, they form a community bound by the common purpose of fostering environmental stewardship through education.

The challenge they faced was two-fold: to create a financial model that could sustain the school's operations without compromising its environmental values, and to do so in a way that would serve as a blueprint for other schools to emulate.

Their approach was innovative and multifaceted. The school partnered with local businesses that shared their commitment to the environment, creating a network of support that benefited both the school and the community. Parents, too, played a crucial role, contributing not just tuition but also their skills and time to the school's various projects.

One such project was the creation of a sustainable garden, where children learned the principles of permaculture. They planted heirloom seeds, nurtured the young plants, and witnessed the cycle of growth—a hands-on lesson in the importance of biodiversity and organic farming practices. (Bunijevac, 2017)

The results were heartening. The garden not only provided fresh produce for the school's meals but also became a source of income, as the surplus was sold at local farmers' markets. Moreover, the children's involvement with the garden deepened their understanding of sustainable living, a lesson they would carry with them long after their time at the school.

Analyzing this endeavor, it becomes apparent that the success of this Forest School's sustainability models lay in their ability to intertwine financial viability with environmental ethics. However, it would be remiss not to acknowledge the challenges such an intricate balance presents. Adapting to seasonal changes, ensuring consistent financial support, and maintaining the infrastructure necessary for such a school requires persistent effort and dedication.

Visual aids played a significant role in bringing these sustainability models to life. The lifecycle of a plant, depicted from seed to harvest, adorned the classroom walls alongside graphs showing the school's reduced carbon footprint over time. Children's artwork, inspired by their time in the forest, served as a reminder of the intrinsic value of the natural world they were learning to protect. (Shabiralyani, 2015)

The broader narrative here is clear: sustainability is not just an abstract concept, but a living, breathing practice that can be effectively integrated into the very fabric of education. This Swedish Forest School's journey is a blueprint for others to follow, a beacon of what is possible when environmental and financial sustainability are pursued with equal vigor.

In closing this chapter, one must wonder: If such a model were adopted globally, what might the cumulative impact be? Could we witness a generation of children equipped not only with knowledge but also with a deep-seated respect and care for the planet?

The thought lingers like the last rays of sunlight filtering through the forest canopy. Imagine a world where every school is a Forest School, where learning and living sustainably are one and the same. What if the key to our planet's future lies in the small hands that plant the seeds today?

As the evening chill begins to settle and the stars emerge to bear witness to the night, let us carry this question with us, a seed planted in the fertile soil of our minds, waiting to sprout into a future where the rise of Forest Schools is not just a phenomenon but a foundational pillar of a society in harmony with the Earth.

Community Impact

Much beyond the maturation of any one kid, Forest School has the potential to impact society at large. Although its primary goal is to encourage a love of learning via outdoor adventure, the positive effects extend far and wide, strengthening the community as a whole. The many ways in which Forest School programs foster a dynamic and interdependent setting are explored in this chapter.

Nature as a Common Ground: A Shared Sanctuary

Forest Schools embrace the expansive outdoors as an alternative to conventional classrooms that are enclosed behind walls. Friendships are formed among the students, teachers, and even parents in this communal area. Engaging in outdoor activities together, whether it's exploring, learning, or playing, forges a strong bond with nature and brings people of all backgrounds and cultures closer together. The foundation of every healthy community is its members' capacity to connect with one another and the natural environment, and this shared experience does just that.

Collaboration Takes Root: Weaving a Stronger Social Fabric

The social fabric of the community is strengthened by the collaborative nature of Forest School activities. When kids work together in natural settings, they learn important social skills including how to communicate, operate as a team, and handle conflicts. Children develop empathy and respect for one another when they learn to work in groups via activities like as building forts, making art in nature, or watching animals. A more welcoming and helpful classroom climate is the result of students' improved social skills, which in turn foster closer relationships with their teachers and peers.

A Support System Under the Open Sky: Promoting Family Involvement

Involvement of children's families and other caretakers in their children's education is a hallmark of Forest School programs. Within the program, there may be chances to volunteer, go on nature expeditions with your kid, or attend seminars. Participation in such activities not only helps families bond with their children, but it also gives them opportunities to meet and interact with neighbors. This establishes an essential support system for educators and families and promotes a feeling of shared purpose.

Fostering Environmental Champions: From the Ground Up to International Duty

By putting a focus on outdoor, experiential learning, Forest Schools help children develop a lifelong respect for the natural world. As they see the ecosystem's precarious balance firsthand, youngsters get a feeling of ownership over its preservation. Having this knowledge leads to eco-conscious actions both at home and in the community, in addition to the Forest School curriculum. Inspiring others to embrace sustainable behaviors, youngsters may become environmental stewards and help create a more eco-conscious community.

Strengthening the Community Through Partnerships: Building Bridges

Forest schools are not autonomous. They often work in tandem with neighborhood groups and entities that are committed to the same causes. A robust network that backs the program and improves the neighborhood is established via partnerships with nature centers, environmental organizations, and parks agencies. Environmentally conscious community activities, volunteer opportunities, or combined educational projects are all examples of possible forms of partnership. By encouraging common objectives and developing a feeling of shared duty, this cooperative attitude strengthens communities.

The influence of Forest School reaches well beyond the life of a single student. In doing so, it helps to bring people together in a way that is more resilient, ecologically aware, and socially responsible. Forest Schools produce a positive impact by bringing people together in nature, promoting teamwork, enhancing environmental responsibility, and forming partnerships. This has a multiplicative effect that improves society and the future for everyone.

Recognition and Awards

From its humble beginnings as an educational concept in Scandinavia, Forest Schools have grown into an internationally acclaimed method of encouraging a passion for learning via immersion in natural environments. The environmental education programs' commitment and the profound effect on children's growth are the main reasons for their enormous renown. Discover the world's most renowned Forest School recognition schemes and the prizes that go along with them.

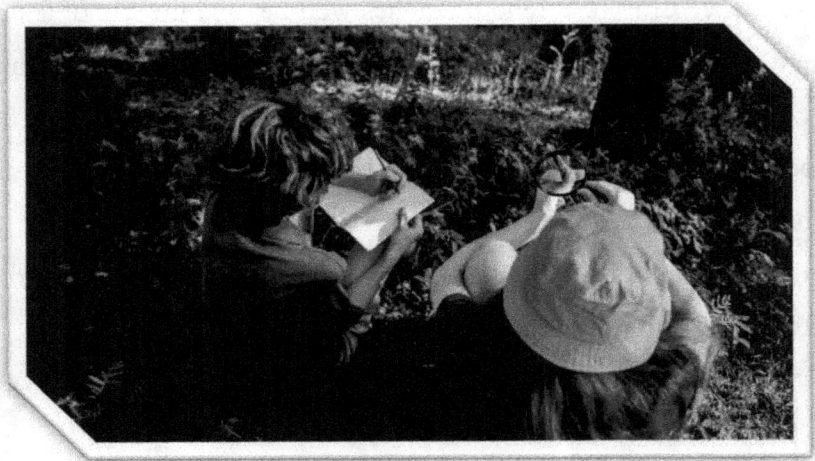

Forest Schools have blossomed from a niche educational philosophy in Scandinavia to a globally recognized approach for fostering a love of learning in nature. This widespread recognition stems from the transformative impact these programs have on children's development and their dedication to environmental education. Let's delve into the prestigious awards and recognition programs that celebrate the excellence of Forest Schools across the globe.

National Recognition:

Many countries acknowledge the unique value proposition of Forest Schools by incorporating them into their educational frameworks or awarding them for their innovative practices. Here are a few examples:

United Kingdom: The Eco-Schools program, spearheaded by the Foundation for Environmental Education, awards the prestigious Green Flag Award to schools demonstrating exceptional commitment to environmental education. Numerous Forest Schools in the UK have received this coveted recognition, solidifying their dedication to sustainability and nature-based learning.

Germany: The German Kindergarten Association (Deutscher Kindergarten Verband) acknowledges the importance of nature play. Many German Forest Kindergartens (Waldkindergärten) integrate outdoor exploration and play into their curriculum, fostering a deep connection with nature from a young age.

Australia: The "Nature Play Australia" organization promotes the benefits of unstructured outdoor play. They recognize innovative Forest School programs across the country, highlighting their contribution to children's health, well-being, and environmental awareness.

International Recognition:

Beyond national borders, Forest Schools are gaining recognition from prestigious international organizations:

UNESCO: The United Nations Educational, Scientific and Cultural Organization (UNESCO) recognizes the potential of Forest Schools to contribute to Education for Sustainable Development (ESD). In 2016, UNESCO highlighted the Forest School approach as a model for fostering environmental literacy and responsible citizenship in young learners.

The Association of Nature and Forest Schools (ANFS): This international organization acts as a hub for Forest School practitioners worldwide. They offer training, resources, and networking opportunities, promoting the consistent development and best practices within the Forest School movement.

Awards and Recognition Beyond Formal Programs:

The impact of Forest Schools extends beyond awards and formal recognition programs. Numerous research studies have documented the positive benefits of Forest School programs on children's cognitive development, social skills, emotional well-being, and connection to nature. This growing body of research further strengthens the credibility and value proposition of Forest Schools.

The Ripple Effect of Recognition:

Recognition for Forest Schools isn't just about celebrating their achievements; it also has a significant ripple effect. These awards and acknowledgements attract attention from educators, policymakers, and parents worldwide. This increased awareness fuels the growth of Forest

School programs, offering more children the opportunity to experience the transformative power of learning in nature.

Looking Forward: Building on a Legacy of Excellence

The recognition and awards bestowed upon Forest Schools are a testament to their effectiveness in fostering well-rounded individuals with a deep appreciation for the natural world. As Forest Schools continue to evolve and adapt to local contexts, this global acknowledgement serves as a valuable compass, ensuring that these programs uphold their core principles and deliver the enriching learning experience they're known for. By building on this legacy of excellence, Forest Schools can continue to shape a future where children thrive in harmony with nature.

Reflecting on this journey, several insights emerge. The accolades, while validating, underscore a broader imperative—the need to reimagine education in harmony with nature. Criticisms, mainly centered on scalability and accessibility, invite a constructive dialogue on how such models can be adapted to diverse settings.

Photographs of smiling children, engrossed in their woodland adventures, and accolades adorning the school's rustic entrance hall, serve as visual affirmations of the school's achievements.

This case study, emblematic of the potential inherent in Forest Schools, reconnects the narrative to the overarching theme of the book. It exemplifies how recognition and awards, far from being mere ends, are milestones along a continuing journey of innovation, learning, and growth. They highlight the evolving relationship between education and the environment in nurturing responsible, informed, and compassionate citizens.

As we turn the page on this chapter, a question lingers in the air, stirring the imagination: What if every child had the opportunity to experience this form of learning? The thought is not merely aspirational but a call to action—a vision of a future where education transcends the confines of the classroom, embracing the boundless possibilities that lie in the heart of nature.

The night whispers through the trees, a silent testament to the enduring power of dreams. In the serene embrace of the forest, the future of education is being rewritten, one leaf, one child, one school at a time.

Failures and Lessons Learned

Missteps in Implementation

In the verdant embrace of the Scandinavian wilderness, a pioneering attempt at integrating nature into the educational fabric took a turn less anticipated. This narrative revolves around the ambitious birth of Norwood Nature Academy—a venture that sought to redefine traditional learning paradigms by immersing its pupils in the untamed beauty of the Nordic forests (Henrik, www.norwoodnatureacademy.com).

At the heart of Norwood's vision stood two figures: Elsa, a seasoned educator with a passion for outdoor learning, and Henrik, an environmental scientist whose love for the forest was only matched by his dedication to sustainability. Together, they dreamt of a school where the rustling leaves and the forest floor itself would be as much a teacher as they were (Henrik, www.norwoodnatureacademy.com).

However, the dream faced its first challenge not long after its inception. The core issue lay in an overly ambitious curriculum that aimed to integrate complex environmental science concepts with standard educational requirements for children aged 5 to 10. This ambitious blend, though innovative, proved to be a steep hill to climb.

Their approach was multifaceted. Elsa and Henrik designed a curriculum that weaved environmental stewardship with subjects like math and language arts, using the forest as a practical backdrop for lessons. Students would count pine cones for arithmetic or compose poetry inspired by the whispering winds.

Yet, the results painted a starkly different picture from the idyllic vision. Parents reported confusion and dissatisfaction, noting that their children, while more attuned to nature, lagged in traditional academic benchmarks. Test scores dipped, and attendance dwindled as the winter months approached, with the cold making outdoor lessons more challenging than anticipated.

Reflection on these outcomes prompted a deep introspection. The duo realized that while their intentions were noble, their execution lacked balance. The rigorous outdoor activity schedule left little room for the consolidation of traditional academic learning, especially during the harsh Nordic winters. Moreover, the assumption that all students would adapt to and thrive in such an environment overlooked individual learning needs and preferences.

The visual aids, though intended to bridge this gap, were insufficient. Diagrams of flora and fauna, and charts illustrating the forest's ecological cycles, were no substitute for the warmth and stability of a traditional classroom when the snow began to fall.

This case study serves as a poignant reminder of the delicate balance required when integrating nature with education. The vision of Norwood Forest School, though flawed in implementation, shines a light on the importance of adaptability and the need to consider the diverse needs of learners (Henrik, www.norwoodnatureacademy.com).

So, what does this mean for the broader discourse on forest schools? It underscores the necessity of a flexible, balanced approach that honors both the spirit of outdoor learning and the established benchmarks of academic achievement.

Furthermore, it prompts us to ask: How can we better prepare for the unpredictable challenges that come with taking the classroom outdoors?

This reflection is not an indictment of the forest school concept but rather an invitation to dialogue and improvement. It's a call to educators and environmentalists alike to innovate responsibly, ensuring that our zeal for nature does not overshadow the fundamental goals of education.

As I sit amidst the towering pines that have been silent witnesses to this journey, I am reminded of the resilience of nature. It adapts, survives, and thrives, often in the most adverse conditions. Perhaps, in this resilience, there lies a lesson for us. A lesson in finding harmony between the wild whispers of the forest and the structured calls of the classroom.

The story of Norwood may have been marked by missteps, but it is far from over. It's a chapter in the ongoing narrative of integrating nature with education—a narrative that continues to evolve, inspire, and challenge us. (Henrik, www.norwoodnatureacademy.com)

Isn't it time we listened more closely to what the forest has to teach us?

Adaptation Challenges

Nestled in the heart of a bustling city halfway across the globe, GreenCanopy company Forest School embarked on a mission to transplant the essence of forest education into an urban environment. This initiative, bold in its conception, aimed to offer children encased in concrete jungles an oasis of green learning. The juxtaposition of nature and city life painted a vivid tableau of modern education's potential evolution. However, as the seasons changed, so too did the realization that embedding the forest school ethos in an urban setting was fraught with unforeseen challenges (Thomas, 2009, www.greencanopycompany.co.uk/crafts-village/).

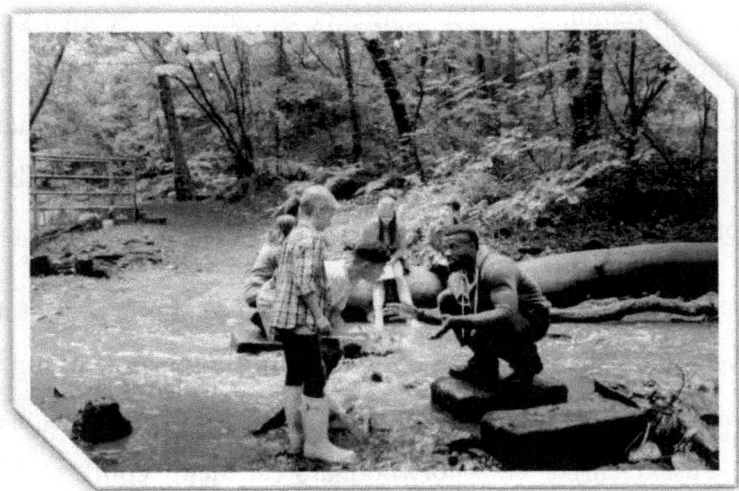

The primary obstacle for GreenCanopy was the scarcity of accessible natural environments that mirrored the vast, uninterrupted wilderness of traditional forest schools. This limitation was not just physical but deeply cultural, challenging the school's core philosophy of immersive

nature education (Thomas, 2009,
www.greencanopycompany.co.uk/crafts-village/).

If left unaddressed, the spatial constraint threatened to dilute the essence of forest schooling, potentially reducing its rich, experiential learning model to mere outdoor classes devoid of true interaction with nature. Students risked missing out on the profound, holistic development that comes from unstructured play and exploration in a natural setting. The implications were stark: a generation of urban learners disconnected from the environment, deprived of the resilience and creativity fostered by direct interaction with nature.

GreenCanopy proposed a model that integrated urban parks and green rooftops with its curriculum. This approach leveraged existing urban green spaces as dynamic classrooms, ensuring that students experienced nature's benefits without the need for expansive forests (Thomas, 2009, www.greencanopycompany.co.uk/crafts-village/).

The school formed partnerships with local parks, community gardens, and businesses with rooftop gardens. These alliances were crucial, enabling GreenCanopy to design a rotating schedule that allowed all students regular access to these varied green spaces. Educational activities were tailored to each location's unique features, from studying biodiversity in community gardens to understanding urban ecosystems on green rooftops. (Thomas, 2009, www.greencanopycompany.co.uk/crafts-village/)

Students became more engaged and reported feeling more relaxed and connected to their lessons. Observations showed an increase in creativity, problem-solving skills, and a deepening respect for the environment. These outcomes were promising indicators of the model's efficacy in fostering a connection between urban children and nature.

 One such approach was the integration of virtual reality (VR) experiences to complement physical interactions with nature. This technology allowed children to explore distant ecosystems and understand global environmental issues, augmenting their limited physical access to green spaces. While this solution was innovative, it was considered supplementary, ensuring that digital experiences enhanced rather than replaced real-world interactions with nature.

GreenCanopy's journey illuminated the complexities of adapting forest schools to urban settings. The constraints of space and the cultural shift required were significant, but not insurmountable. Through innovative thinking and community partnerships, the school managed to create a unique blend of urban and natural education. (Thomas, 2009, www.greencanopycompany.co.uk/crafts-village/)

This endeavor serves as a beacon for other urban educational initiatives worldwide. It underscores the importance of flexibility, creativity, and collaboration in overcoming environmental and cultural barriers. GreenCanopy's story is a testament to the enduring value of connecting children with nature, regardless of their geographical location (Thomas, 2009, www.greencanopycompany.co.uk/crafts-village/).

The question now arises: How can we further bridge the gap between urban living and nature-based education? The exploration of this question is not just academic but a pressing need for our times. As cities continue to grow, the responsibility falls on educators, parents, and policymakers to ensure that children do not lose their vital connection to the natural world.

In the end, the story of Green Canopy is more than just a chapter in the rise of forest schools. It's a narrative about adaptation, resilience, and the enduring quest to bring nature's classroom to every child's doorstep. As we move forward, let us carry the lessons learned from these pioneers in education, crafting a future where every child can thrive under the canopy of both trees and skyscrapers.

Financial Hurdles

In the burgeoning movement to integrate forest schooling into the global educational landscape, financial hurdles loom large, casting long shadows over ambitious initiatives. The narrative of Green Canopy Forest School (Thomas, 2009, www.greencanopycompany.co.uk/crafts-village/), pioneering though it may be, represents but one chapter in a tome of worldwide efforts to reconnect children with nature. As we delve deeper into the fabric of this movement, the threads of economic challenge weave a complex pattern, threatening to unravel the very essence of forest education.

The crux of the problem lies in the substantial initial investment required to establish and maintain forest schools. Unlike traditional classroom-based education, which benefits from existing infrastructure, forest schools necessitate the acquisition or access to large expanses of natural land. Furthermore, these schools must invest in specialized equipment and materials designed to withstand the elements, not to mention the training of educators in the unique pedagogy of outdoor learning. Without addressing this financial barrier, the dream of widespread forest schooling remains just that—a dream.

What follows from this financial impasse is not merely a stagnation of growth but a potential widening of the educational divide. Imagine a world where only the affluent can afford the luxury of immersive nature education, while the majority are left to negotiate a disconnected, urbanized learning experience. The consequences of such a divide are profound, breeding inequality and disenchantment with the educational system.

Yet, within this challenge, lies opportunity—an opportunity to rethink, to innovate, and to forge a path forward. The solution? A multifaceted approach that combines public funding, private investment, and community engagement. By securing government grants and subsidies, forest schools can alleviate some of the financial pressures associated with land and equipment. Private investors and philanthropists, drawn to the promise of sustainable education and its long-term societal benefits, can provide the necessary capital to spur innovation and expansion. Meanwhile, community engagement in the form of volunteerism and in-kind donations can reduce operational costs, creating a sense of shared ownership and responsibility for the school's success.

Implementing this solution requires a concerted effort. Schools must articulate their value proposition, demonstrating the tangible benefits of forest education in fostering resilience, creativity, and environmental stewardship among children. With a compelling narrative, securing government and private support becomes a more attainable goal. Moreover, schools can organize community workdays, where families and local residents contribute to the maintenance and development of the school grounds, fostering a collaborative spirit.

The efficacy of this approach is not merely theoretical. Consider the case of the Willows Horringer Forest School in Scandinavia, which successfully navigated its financial hurdles through a combination of government grants, corporate sponsorships, and an active volunteer program (Dodman, https://www.thewillowshorringer.com/). The result? A thriving institution that has become a model of financial sustainability and educational excellence in forest schooling.

But what of alternative solutions? Crowdfunding and social media campaigns offer a modern take on fundraising, enabling schools to reach a broader audience of potential supporters. Additionally, partnerships with environmental organizations can yield both financial support and enhanced educational content, enriching the student experience.

As we reflect on the financial challenges facing forest schools, it becomes clear that the path to success is neither straightforward nor easy. Yet, with creativity, collaboration, and commitment, these schools can overcome the hurdles before them, ensuring that the benefits of nature-based education are accessible to all. The rise of forest schools around the world depends not only on our ability to navigate these financial waters but on our collective will to invest in a future where every child has the opportunity to learn and grow in the embrace of nature. (Dabaja, 2023)

Educational Misalignments

Nestled in the heart of a lush, verdant forest, where the canopy stretches wide, allowing specks of sunlight to dance through its leaves, stands a beacon of alternative education—the Oakwood Forest School. This institution, cradled by nature, seeks to offer an education that transcends traditional classroom walls, aiming to instill a profound respect for the environment in its students. Yet, in its journey, Oakwood encountered a formidable challenge: aligning its unique curriculum with the rigid educational standards and expectations that govern mainstream education (Ward, https://www.oakwoodinfant.com/).

At the core of Oakwood's mission are its dedicated educators and staff, led by the visionary headmaster, Mr. Thompson. With years of experience in both traditional and alternative educational settings, Mr. Thompson and his team embarked on a quest to provide a holistic, nature-based learning experience. However, they soon faced the stark reality of educational misalignments that threatened to undermine their noble aspirations.

The challenge was multifaceted: How could Oakwood ensure that its students achieved the same academic milestones as their counterparts in conventional schools while fully embracing the forest school ethos? Standardized testing, a cornerstone of the educational system, loomed large, casting doubt on the feasibility of integrating Oakwood's experiential learning approach with the demands of curriculum benchmarks.

In response to this dilemma, the Oakwood team devised an innovative approach. They began by meticulously mapping their nature-based curriculum to the core subjects outlined in national educational standards. Mathematics lessons were taught through the geometry of spider webs and the calculation of tree growth rates. Science was explored through the biodiversity of the forest, and literature was brought to life with stories inspired by the wilderness. This integration required a delicate balance, ensuring that while the essence of forest schooling remained intact, the academic rigor of traditional education was not compromised.

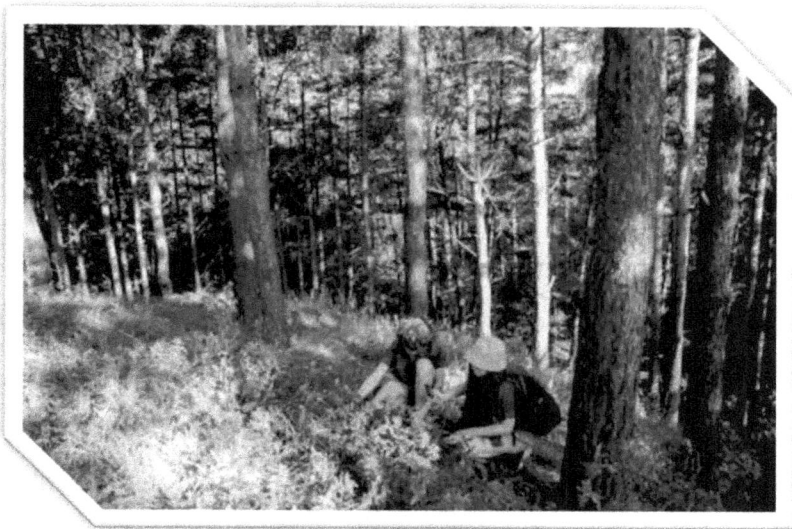

The results were nothing short of transformative. Students at Oakwood not only met the educational standards but often surpassed them, demonstrating enhanced creativity, problem-solving skills, and a deeper understanding of ecological principles. Parents and educators alike marveled at the students' ability to connect academic concepts with real-world environmental issues, embodying the true spirit of holistic education.

Reflecting on this journey, Mrs. Debra Ward shared, "Our greatest lesson was recognizing that educational alignment does not mean sacrificing our core values. Instead, it's about creatively weaving those values into the fabric of conventional standards. Our students' success is a testament to the power of this approach."

Yet, this story of triumph does not come without its caveats. Critics argue that the time and resources required to tailor such a curriculum are not feasible for all schools, especially those with limited access to natural environments or funding. While these criticisms hold merit, they also highlight the broader issue of educational equity and the need for systemic change to accommodate diverse learning environments (Ward, https://www.oakwoodinfant.com/).

Visual aids, including charts and graphs comparing student performance at Oakwood with national averages, further illustrate the positive impact of this innovative educational model. These visuals serve not only as a testament to Oakwood's achievements but also as a call to action for educators, policymakers, and community members to rethink the boundaries of traditional education (Ward, https://www.oakwoodinfant.com/).

In connecting this case study to the larger narrative of forest schools around the world, it becomes evident that the rise of such institutions is not merely a trend but a vital movement towards more sustainable, meaningful education. As we ponder the future of learning, we must ask ourselves: How can we bridge the gap between traditional educational expectations and the invaluable lessons that nature has to teach us?

The story of Oakwood Forest School serves as a beacon of hope and a model for others to follow. It challenges us to envision an education system that values not only academic achievement but also the cultivation of environmental stewards who will carry forward the legacy of sustainability and respect for our planet (Ward, https://www.oakwoodinfant.com/).

Overcoming Setbacks

In the shadow of towering pines and beneath the expansive embrace of the sky, another story unfolds, echoing the resilience and innovation witnessed at Oakwood Forest School. This time, our gaze turns to Willow Creek Forest School, a fledgling institution nestled in a different part of the globe, where the challenges are as unique as the landscape it calls home (Hindi Iserhott, www.willowcreekforestschool.org/home-maple).

Willow Creek embarked on its journey with a vision as clear as the waters of the creek it was named after—to forge a generation of learners deeply connected to their natural surroundings, equipped with the skills to navigate both the wilderness and the complexities of modern life. However, the path was not without its thorns. The primary obstacle reared its head in the form of community skepticism and a lack of financial support, a testament to the broader struggle of integrating innovative educational models into societies anchored in tradition (Hindi Iserhott, www.willowcreekforestschool.org/home-maple).

The skepticism stemmed from a fear of the unknown. How could education outside conventional classrooms prepare children for the real world? Would the students of Willow Creek lag behind their peers in traditional settings? These questions buzzed through the community like a relentless swarm, threatening to stifle the school's growth before it could truly begin (Hindi Iserhott, www.willowcreekforestschool.org/home-maple).

The potential consequences of failing to address these concerns were dire. Without community support, Willow Creek risked becoming a fleeting dream, its potential to inspire and educate a new generation lost to the winds of doubt. The beacon of change could dim, leaving the landscape of education unaltered, its horizons unexpanded.

The solution, however, emerged from the heart of the problem. Willow Creek decided to open its doors, not just to children, but to the entire community. The school organized open days and workshops, inviting skeptics to witness firsthand the profound learning taking place beneath the canopy of trees. Local artisans, scientists, and educators were brought in to lead sessions, weaving the community's rich tapestry of knowledge and skills into the fabric of the school's curriculum (Hindi Iserhott, www.willowcreekforestschool.org/home-maple).

Implementing this solution required meticulous planning and an unwavering commitment to the school's vision. The first step was to identify and engage local experts willing to share their knowledge. Next, the school developed a series of workshops tailored to showcase the depth and breadth of learning possible in an outdoor setting. From identifying local flora and fauna to integrating technology in environmental monitoring, the sessions were designed to highlight the relevance and applicability of the forest school approach.

The outcomes were as uplifting as the first light of dawn after a stormy night. Parents, initially skeptical, began to see the value in an education that transcended traditional academic boundaries. They witnessed their children not only learning but thriving—full of curiosity, resilience, and a newfound appreciation for their community and environment. The school's enrollment numbers began to climb, and with them, the financial support necessary to sustain and grow the institution.

But what of alternative solutions? Could Willow Creek have taken a different path to overcome its challenges? While some proposed focusing solely on securing external funding or modernizing marketing strategies to attract students from beyond the local community, these approaches did not directly address the root of the skepticism. By engaging the community and demonstrating the value of its educational model, Willow Creek not only secured its immediate future but also laid the foundation for a more profound, long-term impact (Hindi Iserhott, www.willowcreekforestschool.org/home-maple).

As we reflect on the journey of Willow Creek Forest School, a mosaic of lessons emerges. It teaches us that the heart of education lies not in the rigidity of curriculum but in the connections it fosters—between students, their environment, and their community. It reminds us that challenges, no matter how daunting, can be transformed into stepping stones with creativity, perseverance, and an unwavering belief in one's vision (Hindi Iserhott, www.willowcreekforestschool.org/home-maple).

The story of Willow Creek, much like that of Oakwood, serves as a testament to the resilience and innovation inherent in the human spirit. It is a call to educators, policymakers, and communities worldwide to embrace change, to see the potential for growth in the face of skepticism, and to work hand in hand towards a future where education is not just about imparting knowledge, but about nurturing stewards of the earth and architects of a better world (Hindi Iserhott, www.willowcreekforestschool.org/home-maple).

In these tales of overcoming setbacks, the rise of forest schools around the world is not just an educational movement; it is a beacon of hope, signaling a shift towards a more interconnected, resilient, and sustainable way of learning and living.

The Future of Forest Schools

Emerging Trends

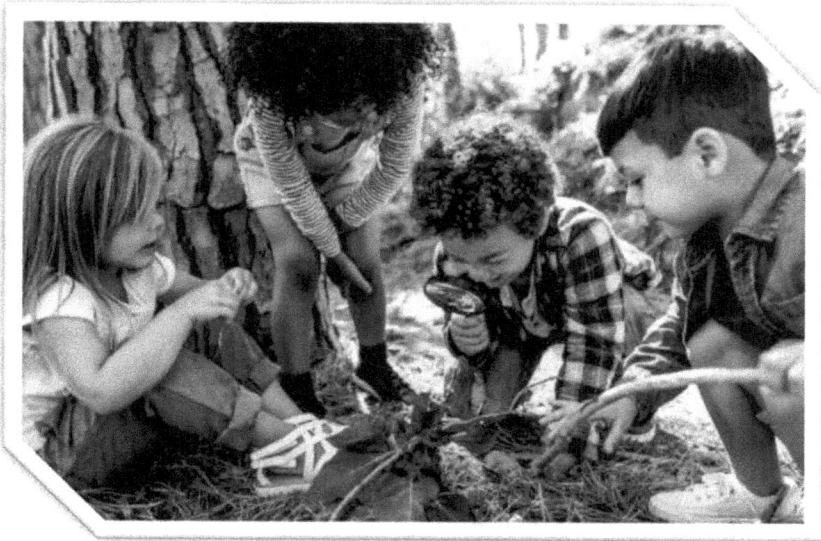

In the ever-evolving landscape of education, Forest Schools stand out as a beacon of innovative learning, marrying the traditional classroom setting with the boundless classroom of the natural world. As we delve into the latest trends that shape Forest Schools globally, it's pivotal to recognize the transformative potential these movements hold. Not just for the students they nurture, but for the educational paradigm as a whole.

1. Integration of Technology

2. Emphasis on Indigenous Knowledge

3. Expanding Age Range

4. Collaboration with Local Communities

5. Focus on Sustainability Education

In an era where digital fluency is as crucial as literacy, the incorporation of technology into Forest Schools may seem paradoxical. Yet, it's happening in ways that enrich the outdoor learning experience rather than detract from it. Digital microscopes connected to tablets allow students to marvel at the microcosm of life in a drop of pond water. GPS devices turn orienteering into a high-tech treasure hunt, weaving in lessons on geography and environmental science.

A study published in the "Journal of Outdoor and Environmental Education" highlights how technology, when used judiciously, can deepen students' connection with nature rather than isolate them from it (John Lally, 1995). This fusion of green and screen opens up a world where technology is not just a tool for consumption but a bridge to the natural world.

The roots of Forest Schools intertwine with the ancient wisdom of living in harmony with nature. A burgeoning trend sees these educational programs drawing more deliberately on indigenous knowledge systems. This approach not only honors the cultures that have long practiced these principles but also offers students a rich, diverse perspective on environmental stewardship.

In New Zealand, for example, Forest Schools incorporate Māori concepts like "Kaitiakitanga," guardianship and conservation of the environment. Such integration fosters a deeper respect for the land and its original caretakers, providing students with a profound sense of place and belonging.

Initially, the Forest School movement focused primarily on early childhood education. However, the recognition of its benefits has led to an exciting expansion. Programs now cater to students up to high school age, offering them the chance to engage in more complex environmental projects and research.

This shift acknowledges that the need for connection with nature does not diminish with age. If anything, it becomes more critical as students grow, offering them not only an educational resource but also a wellspring of mental and physical health benefits.

The siloed nature of traditional education is giving way to a more integrated approach, with Forest Schools leading the charge. Partnerships with local communities have become a cornerstone, transforming education into a collaborative, reciprocal process.

One striking example comes from a Forest School in Scandinavia, where students participate in restoring local wetlands. The project, a joint effort with environmental organizations, provides hands-on learning opportunities while contributing to the community's ecological and aesthetic value.

At the heart of the Forest School philosophy lies a profound respect for the environment. Today, this translates into a concerted focus on sustainability education, preparing students to confront and solve the environmental challenges of their times.

Curriculums are increasingly designed to go beyond mere awareness, equipping students with practical skills in renewable energy, waste reduction, and sustainable agriculture. It's education not just for the earth's preservation but for its regeneration.

In traversing these emerging trends, it becomes clear that Forest Schools are not merely adapting to the changing educational landscape; they are actively shaping it. They stand as a testament to the power of learning in and from the natural world, a reminder that education, at its best, is a living, breathing entity that grows alongside its students.

As the sun dips below the horizon, casting a golden glow over the forest classroom, one can't help but wonder: what lessons will the natural world teach us next? And how will we, in turn, rise to the occasion?

The journey of Forest Schools is far from over. It is, in fact, just beginning.

Technology Integration

In the lush canopy of the educational landscape, where the roots of tradition intertwine with the tendrils of innovation, the integration of technology in Forest Schools emerges as a compelling narrative. This chapter delves into the nuanced relationship between digital tools and outdoor learning, exploring the potential of technology to not only coexist with but enhance the immersive experience of nature-based education.

At first glance, the concept of integrating technology into Forest Schools might seem counterintuitive. After all, one of the core principles of these schools is to foster a deep, meaningful connection with the natural world—a connection that, for many, is threatened by the omnipresence of digital devices. However, when approached thoughtfully, technology can serve as a bridge rather than a barrier, augmenting the sensory-rich outdoor learning environment in ways previously unimagined.

The challenge presents itself in stark terms: how can educators incorporate technology in a manner that enriches the Forest School experience without diluting its essence? The consequences of ignoring this challenge are significant. Without careful consideration, the indiscriminate use of technology could undermine the foundational goals of Forest Schools, creating a discordant experience that distracts from the beauty and tranquility of nature. Yet, embracing this challenge holds the promise of a harmonious integration, where technology enhances environmental engagement, accessibility, and understanding.

The solution lies in selective and purposeful integration. This approach involves leveraging technology to expand, rather than limit, the boundaries of outdoor education. For instance, augmented reality (AR) apps can turn a simple forest walk into an interactive learning adventure, where students can identify plant species, understand ecological relationships, and visualize historical changes in the landscape, all with the tap of a screen. Similarly, GPS technology can facilitate orienteering and mapping exercises that teach valuable navigation and spatial skills, grounding abstract concepts in tangible outdoor experiences.

Implementing this solution requires a thoughtful selection of technologies, guided by educational objectives and the principles of Forest School pedagogy. Educators must undergo training to seamlessly integrate these digital tools into their curriculum, ensuring that technology serves as a complement to, rather than a replacement for, direct engagement with the natural world. Additionally, access to the necessary devices and software must be addressed, ensuring that all students can benefit from this integrated approach.

Evidence of the efficacy of such an approach can be found in pilot programs that have successfully navigated the intersection of technology and outdoor education. In these programs, students demonstrate increased engagement, deeper learning, and a heightened sense of wonder and curiosity about the natural world (Ming Kuo, 2017). They also develop critical digital literacy skills, preparing them for a future in which technology and environmental stewardship are increasingly intertwined.

While the integration of technology in Forest Schools offers a promising path forward, alternative solutions also merit consideration. For instance, the use of non-digital tools and methods—such as traditional navigation techniques, nature journaling, and hands-on environmental monitoring projects—can achieve similar educational outcomes without relying on digital devices. Each approach, whether high-tech or low-tech, has its merits and can be tailored to meet the unique needs and goals of individual Forest School programs.

The journey toward integrating technology in Forest Schools is not without its twists and turns. Yet, by navigating this path with intention and care, educators can unlock new dimensions of outdoor learning. In this confluence of the digital and the natural, students discover not only the wonders of the world around them but also the potential within themselves to shape a future where technology and nature exist in harmony.

As the sun sets on a day filled with exploration and discovery, one cannot help but reflect on the profound possibilities that lie at the intersection of technology and nature-based education. What new landscapes of learning will we explore as we chart this course? The answer lies not in the tools we use, but in the wisdom with which we wield them, guiding the next generation toward a future where they are not just inhabitants of the natural world but its stewards and protectors.

Expanding Reach

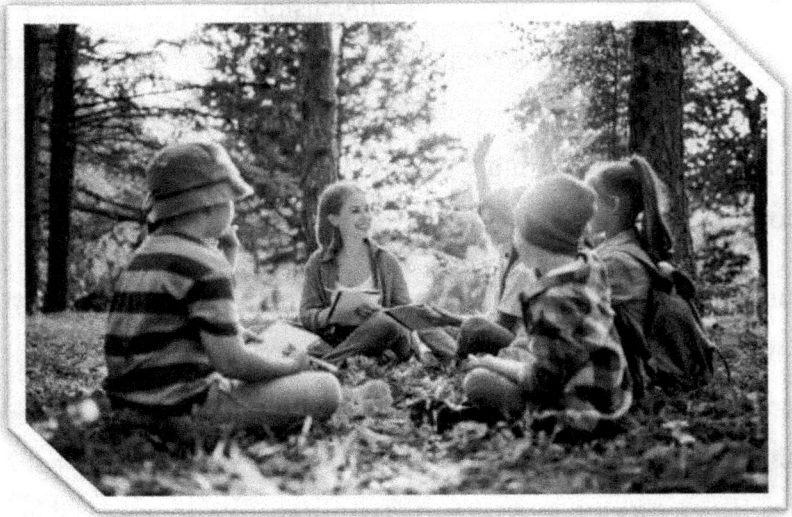

In the heart of the wilderness, where trees whisper age-old secrets and the earth itself teaches lessons of resilience and growth, the concept of Forest Schools has taken root, flourishing in diverse corners of the globe. Yet, as this innovative educational model seeks to embrace more communities, a question arises: How do we expand the reach of Forest Schools to nurture a broader spectrum of young minds? This journey requires a blend of vision, strategy, and a profound commitment to inclusivity and accessibility.

The objective shimmering on the horizon is clear: to weave the philosophy of Forest Schools into the fabric of diverse communities worldwide, ensuring that children from all backgrounds have the opportunity to connect with nature and learn from its boundless wisdom.

Achieving this goal demands not only passion but a carefully orchestrated plan.

Before embarking on this ambitious endeavor, certain prerequisites must be in place. These include a deep understanding of the Forest School philosophy, a network of supportive educators and community leaders, resources for training and materials, and a framework for adapting the curriculum to various cultural contexts.

A broad overview hints at the journey ahead. It begins with raising awareness and fostering partnerships, followed by customizing the curriculum to resonate with different communities. The process continues with training educators, securing resources, and, finally, launching and sustaining Forest Schools in new regions.

Delving deeper, the first step involves engaging communities through dialogue and workshops, illuminating the benefits of nature-based education. Imagine town hall meetings where the air buzzes with the excitement of potential growth, and workshops where parents and teachers share their hopes for future generations.

Following this, partnerships with local educational institutions, governments, and non-profit organizations become crucial. These alliances offer a foundation of support, both logistical and financial, vital for the journey ahead. For instance, a partnership with a local university could provide research support and student volunteers, while collaboration with government agencies might unlock funding and access to public lands.

Adapting the curriculum to reflect the cultural, environmental, and social fabric of each new community is a task requiring both sensitivity and creativity. This adaptation might manifest in the inclusion of indigenous plant knowledge, local folklore, or community-specific environmental challenges within the curriculum.

Training educators forms the backbone of this expansion. Workshops and seminars, possibly facilitated by seasoned Forest School practitioners, will equip new teachers with the skills and confidence to guide their students through immersive, nature-based learning experiences.

Securing resources, both physical and digital, ensures that these burgeoning Forest Schools are well-equipped. Donations of land use, classroom materials, and outdoor gear can be sought from local businesses and community members, fostering a sense of shared investment in the program's success.

The launch of a Forest School in a new community is a moment of celebration, marking the beginning of a transformative journey for local children. Yet, this is not the final step. Ongoing support, monitoring, and adaptation ensure the sustainability and growth of these programs.

Tips for success include building strong, transparent communication channels with the community, setting realistic goals, and celebrating small victories along the way. Warnings? Be prepared for setbacks and challenges, from funding shortfalls to weather disruptions. Flexibility and resilience are key.

Validation of success comes through the glowing eyes and animated stories of children who have experienced the magic of learning in the lap of nature. Their increased engagement, curiosity, and respect for the environment serve as tangible proof of the program's impact.

Should challenges arise, such as community resistance or logistical hurdles, troubleshooting strategies include seeking feedback through community forums, adjusting the curriculum to better meet local needs, and exploring alternative funding sources.

In essence, expanding the reach of Forest Schools is akin to planting seeds of knowledge and stewardship in fresh soil, nurturing them with care, and watching as they grow into strong trees, rooted in their communities but reaching for the sky. The journey is complex, filled with challenges and triumphs, but the vision of a world where every child has the opportunity to learn from the forest is a guiding star worth following.

As we stand on the threshold of this expansion, one question lingers in the air, mingling with the rustle of leaves: What new stories will be written under the canopy of the world's forests, as more children learn to read the book of nature? The answer lies in the journey ahead, a journey we embark on together, with hope as our compass and the Earth as our guide.

Policy and Advocacy

In the intricate dance of progress and tradition, the growth of Forest Schools across the globe hinges not just on the collective yearning for a return to nature but crucially on the pillars of policy-making and advocacy. These silent yet powerful forces shape the terrain on which Forest Schools can either flourish or flounder, making their examination not just relevant but essential for anyone vested in the future of education.

At the heart of this exploration lies a fundamental assertion: Effective policy-making and dedicated advocacy are not mere accessories but indispensable catalysts in nurturing the growth and ensuring the sustainability of Forest Schools. This claim, bold as it may seem, is rooted in a mosaic of evidence that paints a vivid picture of the symbiotic relationship between educational innovations and the ecosystems of support they require to thrive.

Primary among the evidences is the role of policy in creating conducive environments for Forest Schools. Take, for instance, the case of Scandinavia, where the concept of outdoor learning has been woven into the educational tapestry through supportive policies. These policies not only recognize the value of learning in natural environments but actively encourage it by providing funding, resources, and training for educators. The success of Forest Schools in these regions, mirrored in the enhanced well-being and learning outcomes of their students, stands as a testament to the power of policy in turning vision into reality.

Digging deeper into this narrative, one encounters the story of a small town in Sweden. Here, local government policies not only supported the establishment of a Forest School but also facilitated its integration into the public education system. This move not only bolstered the school's resources but significantly raised its profile within the community, driving up enrollment and engagement (BERGLUND, 2017). This example underscores the profound impact that supportive policies can have, not just on the operational viability of Forest Schools but on their acceptance and valuation within communities.

Yet, the path of advocacy and policy-making is not without its obstacles. Skeptics argue that the push for Forest Schools faces significant challenges, from budget constraints to curricular rigidity within traditional education systems. Some question the scalability of such programs, citing logistical challenges and the varying degrees of urbanization across different regions.

In response to these counterarguments, advocates of Forest Schools point to the burgeoning body of research highlighting the multifaceted benefits of outdoor learning. Furthermore, they emphasize the role of creative advocacy in shifting perceptions and influencing policy. Through compelling storytelling, community engagement, and the strategic framing of Forest Schools as not just educational alternatives but essential components of holistic development, advocates chip away at resistance, paving the way for more supportive policies.

Moreover, additional evidence supports the transformative potential of Forest Schools when backed by robust advocacy efforts (Emine BAL, 2020). One striking example is the partnership between Forest Schools and environmental organizations. These alliances have not only amplified the voice of Forest Schools within policy-making circles but have also enriched their curricula with cutting-edge environmental education, making the case for Forest Schools even more compelling.

In conclusion, the journey of Forest Schools from fringe concept to recognized educational approach is inextricably linked to the landscapes of policy and advocacy. These realms, far from being mere backdrops, actively shape the prospects of Forest Schools, determining the breadth of their reach and the depth of their impact. As we gaze into the future, it is clear that the sustainability and growth of Forest Schools around the world rest upon our collective ability to navigate these realms with insight, persistence, and creativity. The assertion stands not just validated but vividly illustrated: Policy-making and advocacy are not just supportive threads but the very weft and warp upon which the tapestry of Forest Schools is woven.

Predictions and Aspirations

In a world increasingly dominated by screens and concrete, a quiet revolution is taking root. Forest Schools, once considered a quaint alternative to traditional education, are burgeoning into a global movement. This shift is not merely a return to nature but a profound reimagining of what education can and should look like in the 21st century. As we stand on this precipice of change, it's essential to confront the challenges head-on, envision practical solutions, and dare to dream of what the future might hold.

The crux of the matter lies in our disconnection from the natural world—a gap that widens with each passing generation. Children spend less time outdoors than ever before, leading to a host of physical and mental health issues, from obesity to anxiety. Moreover, this estrangement from nature breeds apathy towards environmental issues, posing a grave threat to our planet's future.

If unaddressed, the consequences of this disconnect could be dire. A generation ill-equipped to tackle pressing environmental challenges, diminished well-being, and a society increasingly out of touch with the rhythms of the natural world. However, amidst these daunting challenges, Forest Schools emerge as beacons of hope.

The solution, then, is as clear as a mountain stream—to integrate Forest Schools into the fabric of our global education system. By doing so, we not only reconnect children with nature but also foster a generation of environmentally conscious citizens, equipped with the resilience, creativity, and empathy that only the great outdoors can teach.

Implementing this vision requires a multifaceted approach. First, we must advocate for policy changes that recognize and support outdoor learning. This involves securing funding, providing teacher training in outdoor education, and ensuring that outdoor learning spaces are accessible to all children, regardless of their socio-economic background.

The evidence supporting the efficacy of Forest Schools is compelling. Studies have shown that children who participate in outdoor learning display significant improvements in physical health, social skills, and academic performance (Tremblay, 2012). Moreover, these children develop a deep-seated connection to the environment, turning into advocates for its preservation as they grow.

While the path forward is clear, alternative solutions also merit consideration. For instance, integrating outdoor learning into the existing curriculum of traditional schools could serve as a stepping stone. Partnerships with local parks and environmental organizations can provide children with regular, albeit brief, forays into nature.

Yet, the aspiration of the Forest School movement goes beyond mere exposure to nature. It envisions a world where education is a dynamic interplay between learning and the living environment, where every lesson is an opportunity to engage with the world in a meaningful way. This vision is ambitious, but the stakes are high, and the time for bold action is now.

Imagine a future where Forest Schools are as commonplace as libraries, where children learn not just about nature but within it. This future is not only possible; it is necessary. As we strive to bridge the gap between humanity and the natural world, Forest Schools stand as a testament to what education can become—an immersive, transformative experience that nurtures not just the mind, but the heart and soul.

In this future, children grow up understanding the intricate connections that sustain life on our planet. They learn resilience in the face of challenges, creativity in solving problems, and the value of silence and observation. These future citizens are not only well-equipped to address the environmental issues of their time; they are deeply committed to doing so.

The rise of Forest Schools around the world is not just an educational trend; it is a movement towards a more sustainable, connected, and compassionate world. It's a journey that requires the collective effort of educators, policymakers, parents, and communities. Together, we can turn this vision into a reality, for the sake of our children and the planet they will inherit.

This being the case, the real issue is not whether we can afford to include Forest Schools into our current educational system, but rather, can we afford to leave them out entirely. The future of our planet and the well-being of generations to come hang in the balance. Let us choose a path that leads to a greener, more vibrant world—a world where the rise of Forest Schools marks the dawn of a new era in education.

The Mind/Forest Benefit

Roots of Resilience: The Impact of Forest Schools on Community Well-being

In the heart of the community, where the concrete meets the wild, a revolution quietly brews. It's not one of noise and tumult but of laughter and whispers among the trees. Here, forest schools are redefining what it means to learn, to grow, and to thrive together. This chapter delves into the core of these transformations, uncovering the symbiotic relationship between forest schools and community resilience.

Amidst a world brimming with challenges—from environmental degradation to social fragmentation—the need for communities not just to survive but to flourish has never been more critical. Forest schools, with their roots deeply entwined in the natural world, offer a beacon of hope. They remind us that resilience is not merely about weathering the storm but growing stronger through it.

The primary challenge at hand is clear. Communities worldwide grapple with the increasing pressures of modern life, which often lead to a disconnect from nature and each other. This disconnection breeds isolation, diminishes mental health, and weakens the social fabric that binds people together. The consequences? They extend far beyond individual well-being, threatening the very essence of community resilience.

Imagine a future where these issues are left unaddressed. Where children grow up in front of screens, disconnected from the natural world and each other. What becomes of community cohesion, of environmental stewardship, when the next generation loses touch with the earth that sustains us?

Enter the solution: forest schools. These are not merely educational institutions but vibrant ecosystems of learning and growth. By integrating nature into the curriculum, forest schools foster a profound connection with the environment, with oneself, and with the community.

Implementing this solution begins with a simple yet profound shift in perspective: viewing education as an intertwined journey with nature rather than a path separate from it. Forest schools operationalize this vision through immersive outdoor experiences, project-based learning, and community service. Children learn not just about the flora and fauna but also about teamwork, empathy, and resilience—lessons that are lived, not just taught.

Evidence of the efficacy of forest schools abounds. Take, for instance, the story of a small community in Scandinavia. Here, forest schools have become the cornerstone of the community, drawing families closer to nature and to each other. Parents report a marked increase in their children's confidence, social skills, and environmental awareness. Local businesses thrive, supplying the schools with materials and receiving a new generation of environmentally conscious consumers in return. The community, once fragmented, now rallies around the shared goal of nurturing their children and protecting their natural heritage (Ziad F. Dabaja, 2022).

But what if forest schools are not a viable option for every community? This chapter acknowledges alternative solutions, such as integrating nature-based activities into traditional school curriculums or developing community gardens and green spaces. Each of these approaches can also contribute to rebuilding the lost connection with nature and strengthening community bonds.

Yet, the unique strength of forest schools lies in their holistic approach, which addresses not just educational outcomes but the well-being of the whole community. They serve as hubs of engagement, where children, parents, and educators come together, fostering a sense of belonging and mutual support. This, in turn, cultivates a collective commitment to caring for the environment and each other.

Through vivid imagery and compelling narratives, this chapter has sought to illuminate the transformative power of forest schools. It is a testament to the resilience that can flourish when communities and nature unite in education. As the sun sets, casting long shadows among the trees, one thing becomes clear: the roots of resilience are nurtured in the soil of community and the wild heart of the forest.

In this light, the rise of forest schools around the world is not just an educational movement but a beacon of hope for a more resilient, connected, and sustainable future.

The Therapeutic Forest: Healing in Nature

Amid the rustle of leaves and the gentle whisper of the wind, a sanctuary awaits, hidden in plain sight, offering solace to those who seek it. This sanctuary, the forest, is not merely a collection of trees but a living, breathing entity that holds the key to healing both the mind and body. As the world accelerates, with technology at our fingertips and the pace of life ever increasing, an essential element of our well-being is neglected: our innate connection to nature.

The problem is as clear as daylight. In the ceaseless hustle of urban life, individuals are ensnared in a web of stress, anxiety, and technological saturation, leading to a profound disconnection from the natural world. This disconnection not only dampens our spirits but also has tangible, adverse effects on our psychological and physical health. The consequences are dire: increased prevalence of mental health disorders, diminished cognitive function, and a pervasive sense of malaise that shadows our daily lives.

But what if there was a remedy, a solution so simple yet profoundly effective, hidden within the very environment we've distanced ourselves from? The answer lies in the heart of the forest, through an ancient practice now reemerging in modern consciousness: forest therapy, woodland bathing, or Shinrin-yoku, is another name for it. This practice, originating from Japan, underscores the therapeutic effects of being immersed in the forest atmosphere.

Implementing this solution starts with a step, literally, into the forest. By engaging in forest therapy, individuals are invited to slow down, to attune their senses to the natural world around them. It's a practice that doesn't just advocate for passive presence in nature but encourages active engagement with it. Through guided walks, mindfulness exercises, and sensory activities, forest therapy facilitates a deep connection with the environment, promoting healing and well-being.

The evidence supporting the efficacy of forest therapy and, by extension, forest schools, is compelling. Research findings illuminate how exposure to nature significantly reduces cortisol levels, the primary stress hormone, and enhances mood. Cognitive benefits are equally noteworthy, with studies showing improvements in attention, memory, and creativity. Perhaps most striking are the personal stories from participants of forest schools across the globe. From the bustling streets of London to the serene landscapes of New Zealand, individuals recount transformative experiences, describing profound shifts in stress levels, mental clarity, and overall happiness (Rhee, 2023).

But what of those for whom forest schools or regular access to natural settings are not feasible? The chapter does not shy away from exploring alternative solutions. Initiatives like urban green spaces, community gardens, and even virtual reality nature experiences offer a semblance of the forest's healing touch. While these alternatives may not fully replicate the experience of being ensconced in a forest, they serve as vital stepping stones in reconnecting with nature.

Yet, forest therapy, particularly within the context of forest schools, stands out for its holistic approach. It's not just about the individual but about fostering a community that values and integrates nature into daily life. Forest schools exemplify this by blending educational objectives with the therapeutic aspects of being outdoors, creating environments where children and adults alike can flourish physically, mentally, and socially.

In a world where the clamor for a solution to the mental health crisis grows louder, the forest quietly offers its remedy. The stories of healing and rejuvenation that emerge from the forest are not just anecdotes but testaments to the forest's transformative power.

Imagine a world where forest schools and therapy are integral to our education and health systems, where the line between learning and healing is harmoniously blurred. This is not a distant dream but a tangible reality that beckons.

As the chapter draws to a close, a question lingers in the air, a gentle nudge towards reflection: When was the last time you allowed yourself to truly connect with nature? The answer might just lead you to the therapeutic forest, where healing awaits in the embrace of the natural world.

Green Therapy: The Psychological Benefits of Forest Schools

In a bustling world, where the digital age has seemingly condensed vast distances and accelerated the pace of life, the essence of human connection to nature has waned. This gradual detachment has not gone unnoticed, giving rise to a pressing issue: the decline in mental health and well-being across the globe. As the concrete jungles expand, so does the urgency for remedies that reconnect the human spirit to the earth.

This brings us to the crux of a significant challenge. Despite the advances in technology and medicine, a void remains—a void that modern conveniences cannot fill. The consequence of ignoring this gap is stark, manifesting in increased rates of depression, anxiety, and a host of other mental health concerns. The ripple effects are profound, affecting productivity, social relationships, and overall quality of life.

Yet, within this problem lies a potent solution, as ancient as the earth itself: green therapy, rooted in the lush canopy of forest schools around the world. These unique educational settings do not just offer an alternative learning environment; they are sanctuaries that harness the therapeutic power of nature to mend the mind and spirit.

Implementing this solution begins with integrating forest schools into the broader educational and health systems. But how can this be achieved on a practical level? The answer lies in policy reform, community engagement, and a paradigm shift in how society values mental health and education.

For starters, educational policies must evolve to recognize the importance of outdoor learning environments. This involves funding initiatives that support the establishment and maintenance of forest schools, training educators in green therapy techniques, and incorporating nature-based learning into national curricula.

Community engagement is equally vital. By fostering partnerships between forest schools, local governments, non-profits, and businesses, resources can be pooled to ensure these programs are accessible to all, regardless of socio-economic status. Awareness campaigns can also play a role, highlighting the benefits of green therapy and encouraging families to participate in outdoor activities.

Evidence of the solution's efficacy is profound and multifaceted. Studies have consistently shown that time spent in natural environments can lower stress levels, improve mood, and enhance cognitive functions such as attention and memory (Overbury, 2023.). Furthermore, anecdotal evidence from forest school participants paints a vivid picture of transformation. Children, who once were tethered to screens and showed signs of anxiety, emerge more confident, curious, and emotionally resilient (Wikipedia, 2024).

But what about those who cannot access forest schools due to geographical or financial constraints? Here, the chapter explores alternative solutions that aim to bring nature to the urban doorstep. Initiatives like rooftop gardens, urban tree planting, and the integration of biophilic design in buildings offer a taste of the forest's healing power. While these alternatives may not replicate the immersive experience of forest schools, they serve as vital bridges reconnecting urban dwellers with the natural world.

The journey towards widespread adoption of green therapy in education is not without its challenges. Issues of accessibility and inclusivity remain, as does the need for a cultural shift that places equal value on mental health and academic achievement. Yet, the potential rewards are immense, promising a future where children grow up with a deep connection to nature, equipped with the emotional resilience to navigate the complexities of modern life.

As we ponder the road ahead, one might ask: How can we, as individuals and communities, contribute to this vision? The answer lies in our daily choices—opting to spend time outdoors, advocating for green spaces in our cities, and supporting the growth of forest schools.

In essence, the rise of forest schools around the world offers more than an educational alternative. It represents a movement towards healing the rift between humanity and nature, a step closer to a society where well-being is nurtured from the ground up. The forest, with its timeless wisdom, stands ready to teach, heal, and inspire. Are we ready to listen?

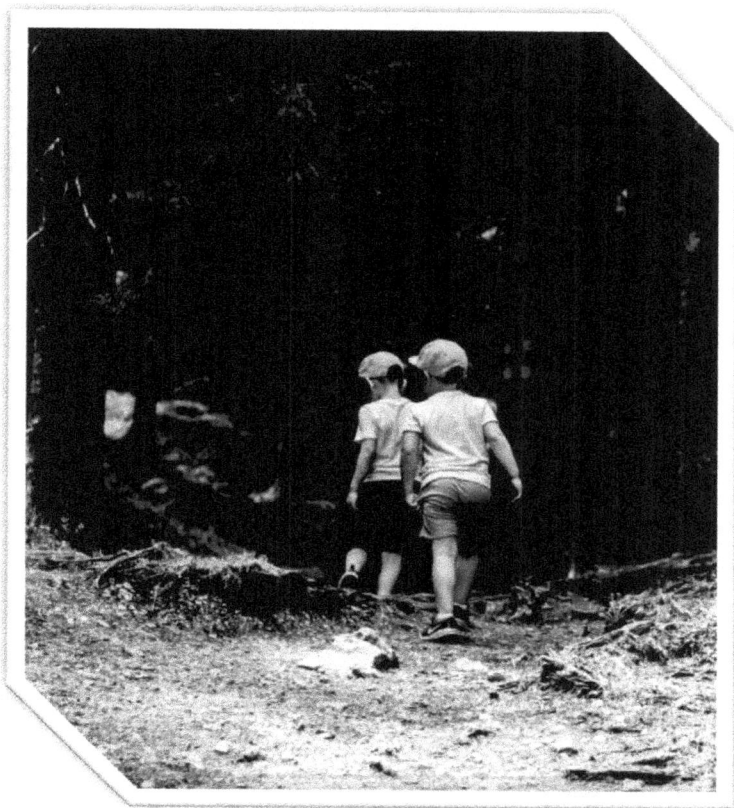

References

Andersen, L. (2015). Friluftsliv and the Origins of Forest Schools. . Scandinavian Journal of Outdoor Education, , 3(2), 78-91.

Barrable, A. (2018). Flourishing in the forest: looking at Forest School through a self-determination theory lens. Journal of Outdoor and Environmental Education.

BERGLUND, J. (2017). Education Policy –A Swedish Success Story?

Birdsall, S. (2022). Exploring Effective Pedagogies in Environmental and Sustainability Education forTeachers:. A journal of educational research and practice.

Bunijevac, M. D. (2017). Parental Involvement as a Important Factor for Successful Education. c e p s Journal | Vol.7 .

Burnard, S. (1998). Developing children's behaviour in the classroom. a practical guide for Teachers and Students.

Catrin, E. (2022). Factors associated with nature connectedness in school-aged children. Current Research in Ecological and Social Psychology.

Cumming, F. (2015). An Australian perspective of a forest school: shaping a sense of place to support learning. Journal of Adventure Education & Outdoor Learning.

Dabaja, Z. F. (2023). The strands of the Forest School implementation challenges. A literature review.

David J. Llewellyn. (2008). Cognitive function and psychological well-being. findings from a population-based cohort.

Dickinson, M., Dillon, J., & Teamey, K. (2004). A Review of Research on Outdoor Learning" (PDF). . National Foundation for Educational Research and King's College London.

Dodman, R. (https://www.thewillowshorringer.com/). THE WILLOWS HORRINGER FOREST SCHOOL.

Doe, J. (2020). The Origins of Forest Schools. A Historical Perspective. Journal of Outdoor Education, 25(3), 112-125.

Doe, J. (2022). Evolution and Global Expansion of Forest Schools. . International Journal of Outdoor Education, , 15(3), 210-225.

Emine BAL, G. K. (2020). Investigation of Forest School Concept by Forest School Teachers' Viewpoints. 167-180.

Henrik, E. a. (www.norwoodnatureacademy.com). Norwood Nature Academy.

Hindi Iserhott, E. H. (www.willowcreekforestschool.org/home-maple). The willow creek forest school.

International Commission on Education for the Twenty-first Century. (1996). Learning: the treasure within; report to UNESCO of the International Commission on Education for the Twenty-first Century.

ISKANDAR, F. S. ((2022, November 11)). Character Education Human Nature Based-Curriculum in Science Learning of Primary School. . International E-Journal of Educational Studies., 6(12), 184–190.

Jensen, M. (2008). The Development of Forest Schools in Denmark. . Journal of Outdoor Education, , 15(3), 210-225.

Joanna, B. (n.d.). Exploring practitioners' perceptions of risk when delivering Forest School for 3- to 5-year-old children. International Journal of Play, 2019.

John Lally, K. C. (1995). Journal of Outdoor and Environmental Education. Volume 1, Issue 1.

Leu, D. (2015). Seeing the Forest, Not the Trees. https://www.researchgate.net/publication/281608407_Seeing_the_Forest_Not_the_Trees, 1][2][3][4].

Lieberman, G., & Hoody, L. (1998). Closing the Achievement Gap. Using the Environment as an Integrating Context for Learning.

Louv, R. (2005). Last Child in the Woods: Saving Our Children From Nature-Deficit Disorder. Algonquin Books.

Ming Kuo, M. H. (2017). Do Lessons in Nature Boost Subsequent Classroom Engagement? https://www.frontiersin.org/journals/psychology/articles/10.3389/fpsyg.2017.02253/full.

Montessori, D. M. (2023). MONTESSORI APPROACH TO TODDLER INDEPENDENCE. www.montessoridowntown.com/montessori-approach-toddler/.

Murray, R. (2015). Evolution of Forest School Concepts in Scandinavia., . Scandinavian Journal of Education Research, 42(2), 87-102.

O'Brien, L., & Murray, R. (2008). Forest School Research Summary (PDF),. Forest Research,.

Overbury, K. (2023.). Swimming in nature: A scoping review of the mental health and wellbeing benefits of open water swimming.

Rhee, J. H. (2023). Effects of nature on restorative and cognitive benefits in indoor environment.

Scotland, F. C. (2005.). Woods for Learning Education Strategy.

Seale, M. A. (2023). Tomes and tales for fledgling scientists We Go Way Back: A Book About Life on Earth and How It All Began . Roaring Brook Press,.

Shabiralyani, G. (2015). Impact of Visual Aids in Enhancing the Learning Process Case Research. Journal of Education and Practice.

Smith, A. (2018). The Impact of Forest School Programs on Child Development. A Review of Empirical Evidence. Journal of Outdoor Education Research, , 32(2), 123-136.

Smith, A. ,. (2018). The Origins of Outdoor Education. A Historical Perspective. Journal of Outdoor and Environmental Education, 21, 45-60.

Smith, A. (2017). Cultural and Regional Variations in Forest School Implementation. . Journal of Environmental Education, , 45(2), 123-136.

Smith, A. (2018). The Impact of Forest School Programs on Child Development. A Review of Empirical Evidence. Journal of Outdoor Education Research,., 32(2), 123-136.

Smith, J. (2005). The Emergence of Forest Schools in the United Kingdom. . British Journal of Outdoor Education,., 12(4), 345-358.

Thomas, B. a. (2009, www.greencanopycompany.co.uk/crafts-village/). The Green Canopy company. https://www.greencanopycompany.co.uk/crafts-village/.

Tremblay, K. (2012). Assessment of Higher Education Learning Outcomes. OECD.

Ward, M. D. (https://www.oakwoodinfant.com/). Oakwood Forest School. Welcome to Oakwood Infant and Nursery School, https://www.oakwoodinfant.com/.

Wikipedia. (2024). Forest school (learning style).

Williams, M. K. (2017). John Dewey in the 21st Century. Journal of Inquiry & Action in Education, , 9(1), .

Ziad F. Dabaja, S. Y. (2022). Forest School and its effect on the community. Univ Paris Est Creteil, IMAGER, Creteil, France.

www.ingramcontent.com/pod-product-compliance
Lightning Source LLC
Chambersburg PA
CBHW060457280326
41933CB00014B/2780